ASK A LAWYER
Debt and Bankruptcy

1|99

D0681531

WITHDRAWN

ALSO BY STEVEN D. STRAUSS

the *Ask a Lawyer* series

Divorce and Child Custody

Landlord and Tenant

Wills and Trusts

ASK A LAWYER

DEBT AND BANKRUPTCY

Steven D. Strauss

W · W · NORTON & COMPANY

NEW YORK   LONDON

For information about permission to reproduce selections from this book,
write to: Permissions, W. W. Norton & Company, Inc., 500 Fifth Avenue,
New York, NY 10110.

The text of this book is composed in Berkeley Book, with the display set in
Futura. Desktop composition by Chelsea Dippel. Manufacturing by the Haddon
Craftsmen, Inc. Book design by Margaret Wagner.

Library of Congress Cataloging-in-Publication Data

Strauss, Steven D., 1958–
    Ask a lawyer. Debt and bankruptcy / Steven D. Strauss.
        p. cm.
    Includes index.
    ISBN 0-393-04586-2. — ISBN 0-393-31731-5 (pbk.)
    1. Bankruptcy—United States—Popular works. 2. Debtor and creditor—
United States—Popular Works. I. Title.
KF1524.6.S765 1998
346.7307'8—dc21   97-30779
                                                               CIP

W. W. Norton & Company, Inc. 500 Fifth Avenue, New York, N.Y. 10110
http://www.wwnorton.com

W. W. Norton & Company Ltd., 10 Coptic Street, London WC1A 1PU

1 2 3 4 5 6 7 8 9 0

This book is dedicated to my wonderful mother, Sandi Strauss, who taught me how to use my heart, and in loving memory of my father, Marty Strauss, who taught me how to use my brain.

For their expertise and guidance with the preparation of this book, many thanks to David Cusick and Stephen Reynolds. I would also like to thank Peter Clevenger, and especially Patricia Chui and Starling Lawrence, for making dreams come true.

CONTENTS

INTRODUCTION: ABOUT THIS BOOK AND THE
ASK A LAWYER SERIES

A person usually needs an attorney to either act as an advocate or provide advice. While there are many books on the market which endeavor to teach people how to be their own lawyer-advocate, this is not one of them. This book, and the *Ask a Lawyer* series, focuses upon the second function of an attorney: dispensing helpful, useful, and needed legal advice.

Few people can afford to pay $250 to sit down with an attorney for an hour in order to get legal help. The *Ask a Lawyer* series is designed to provide the advice of an attorney at a fraction of the cost. Helping people understand the law and their rights; explaining which of several options may work best for them; giving insights, tips, and helpful hints—in short, giving readers the type of assistance that they would expect if they sat down with an expensive lawyer—*is* the purpose of this book and this series.

Money issues in particular are an area of the law that require good, affordable legal help. As this book explains, there are many different possible solutions to financial problems. Not knowing what your options are, or choosing the wrong option, can have catastrophic consequences: losing a home, or even a job. This book will help you figure out which solution makes the most sense for you. How do you get a creditor to stop calling you at work? Should you file for bankruptcy, and if so, what kind of bankruptcy? Will you be able to keep your property? Read on.

This book will sensibly walk you through various solutions to your debt problems. It will caution you about possible pitfalls, explain in simple terms important aspects of the law, and guide you toward a sensible solution to your particular problem.

The book is organized so as to make this often complicated area of the law quite easy to understand. Each chapter has its own outline so that once you turn to a chapter of interest to you, you can quickly find the specific area with which you need help. If, for example, you have a question about protecting personal property in a Chapter 7 bankruptcy, flip to chapter 7, "Protecting Your Personal Property," and look under "What property is exempt?" Each chapter closes with the important legal concept to remember for that chapter so that you leave the topic understanding exactly what it is you need to know.

Appendix A lists many common questions, along with sensible, simple answers. Any **boldface** word in this book can be found in the glossary, Appendix B.

No book of advice can come with a guarantee, and no book can substitute for the advice of an attorney familiar with your particular problems and issues. What this book can do is save you thousands of dollars throughout this process. Absent many hours with high-priced legal counsel, this book is just about the next best thing.

I

GETTING YOUR FINANCIAL HOUSE IN ORDER

EVERYTHING WILL BE ALL RIGHT

Retribution versus forgiveness
Choosing a path

RETRIBUTION VERSUS FORGIVENESS. The law is filled with rage. Most statutes, cases, lawsuits, and court opinions are intended to resolve angry controversies, ultimately resulting in someone being punished: the embezzler is sent to jail, the oil company pays a huge fine, the husband is denied visitation. Someone pays. Consider the following example:

> Distraught over his impending divorce and the realization that he would be seeing far less of his two sons, Grant was hardly paying attention when his car rammed into the side of Shelly's car. Shelly sued Grant, and the jury awarded her $100,000 in damages. Grant was not only alone now, but broke too.
>
> He started drinking too much, was fired from his job, and began to live off of his credit cards. By the time he had pulled himself back from the abyss two years later, Grant was another $100,000 in debt.

Grant could spend the rest of his natural days paying back his creditors, and have nothing to show for it, save a modicum of self-respect. If he failed to repay his debts, his creditors would surely **sue**. Grant would quickly learn that much of the law is indeed about revenge.

That is, except **bankruptcy**. Bankruptcy is the only area of the law that is more concerned with forgiveness than with retribution. Instead of facing nasty lawsuits and vengeance-seeking creditors, bankruptcy allows debtors like Grant to have their debts wiped out, **discharged,** and ultimately forgiven. In bankruptcy, the financial slate is wiped clean, allowing for a **fresh start**.

And it is not just forgiveness of debts that bankruptcy permits; it is the failings of the spirit that are forgiven too. The bankruptcy code does not care *why* a person may be broke. Losing a job is equal to binge buying is equal to poor planning. Anyone who needs it can get a fresh start. A new beginning. A chance to start over. A rare thing, forgiveness.

> After he had sobered up, Grant went to an attorney and discovered that his entire $200,000 in debts could be completely eliminated in a Chapter 7 bankruptcy. Grant filed his paperwork a few days later, and four months later the entire amount was discharged (wiped out). This gave Grant the incentive to start anew. Within a few months, he was working again and spending time with his boys.

CHOOSING A PATH. While your money problems may seem insurmountable, the truth is, they are not. Solutions—viable, simple, affordable solutions—do exist. The solution to your particular problem may involve bankruptcy or it may not. There are other possibilities aside from bankruptcy that can be utilized to right the financial ship; bankruptcy is just the most common and widespread. The important thing to understand is that *there is a way out.*

What are those options? It all depends upon the nature and severity of your problem. If the issue is simply a bad credit rating, then your best course of action is to try to repair your credit file (see chapter 4, "Cleaning Up Your Credit Report"). If a creditor is harassing you, then, surprisingly, a simple letter can put an end to it (see chapter 3, "Dealing with Creditors and Collection Agencies"). If you are behind on a mortgage or car loan, and a **foreclosure** or **repossession** seems inevitable, then a **Chapter 13** bankruptcy is probably your best bet (see section IV, "Chapter 13 Bankruptcy"). If you simply have too much debt and need a chance to start over, then a **Chapter 7** bankruptcy is the way to go (see section III, "Chapter 7 Bankruptcy").

The point is, you do not have to suffer any longer. Ample solutions exist. You can get out from under your personal mountain of debt and get a fresh financial beginning. Take a deep breath and get a good night's sleep. An answer is at hand.

The Important Legal Concept to Remember: To err is human, to forgive, divine. Whether through bankruptcy or some other legal method, solutions to a financial crisis exist.

2

OPTIONS BESIDES BANKRUPTCY

Consumer Credit Counseling
Consolidation loans
Negotiated settlements
Do nothing

When financial circumstances dictate an immediate solution, a Chapter 7 bankruptcy, which offers the chance to make a fresh start and completely wipe out most debts, often makes the most sense. However, that solution has drawbacks that cause some people to consider other options.

CONSUMER CREDIT COUNSELING. Consumer Credit Counseling Service (CCC) is an organization, available in most communities, that helps people restructure their debts.

Because CCC is a nonprofit organization, its fees are very reasonable to you, the **debtor**, and sometimes even free. It is important to realize that CCC *cannot exist* on the amount debtors pay for its service. Who, then, pays the bills at CCC? The credit card companies. CCC is financed by credit card companies and various large retailers. This is good to know. While the credit counselor CCC assigns to you will certainly have your best interests at heart, just remember who pays your counselor's salary.

Your CCC counselor will meet with you a few times in order to go over your debts and income, and help you put together a budget. The counselor will also negotiate on your behalf with your **creditors** in an effort to get your payments down to a manageable level. He does so by getting your creditors to reduce their interest payments and extend the amount of time you have to pay them back. What the counselor will ultimately try to do is create a repayment plan that you can live with.

Rebecca had $10,000 in credit card debt. She found paying the 20 percent interest, and the corresponding $400 total payment, too difficult to meet each month. She went to CCC, and her counselor was able to put together a plan that allowed her to reduce her interest rate to 10 percent and her payments down to a manageable $250 a month. It took Rebecca almost four years to pay the money back, but she did it.

A CCC plan is not for everyone. Depending upon your debt, income, and circumstances, even the negotiated **settlement** amount may be too much to pay every month, or the payment plan may take too long. Also, in most cases, you cannot use any of your credit cards while you are paying off the plan. Nevertheless, when compared to having a bankruptcy on your credit report, which will stay there for ten years, a CCC repayment plan may make sense.

CONSOLIDATION LOANS. Another option may be some type of debt consolidation loan. Such loans can be in the form of a **second mortgage** or a **home equity loan**, an unsecured line of credit from a bank, or a credit card consolidation. While at first blush these consolidation loans may look attractive, the truth is, you should be *extremely wary* of this choice.

Ethel was a widow in her sixties. She had five credit cards with a total debt of about $15,000. One of her credit card companies offered her the chance to consolidate all of her debt on their card at 7 percent interest. A year after she had accepted their offer, the interest rate on the card jumped to 21 percent, and Ethel was back where she started.

Credit card consolidations usually end up being a temporary solution to a permanent problem. Debtors swap one debt for another, without clearing up either. Most debtors who consolidate their credit card debt, in an effort to reduce the entire amount of their overall **indebtedness**, eventually must find a better solution.

You may be surprised to learn that an even worse consolidation option is a home equity loan. Because many lenders are happy to lend you money based upon the **equity** in your home (or car), understanding the concept of equity is important. Equity is the amount of money you would receive if you were to sell your property and pay off the lender(s).

Jillian's house was worth $100,000, and she owed the bank $75,000. She has $25,000 worth of equity in her house. Jillian also has a car worth $10,000, and owes $9,000 on it. She has $1,000 worth of equity in her car.

To understand why the home equity loan option looks better than it actually is, you must also understand the difference between secured and unsecured debts.

A **secured debt** is one that is tied to some sort of collateral. For example, a bank would be happy to loan you the $15,000 you need to buy a used car, but only so long as it holds title to the car until you repay the loan. If you do not pay the bank back, it will repossess the car. The car, the **collateral**, secures the loan. That is a secured debt.

Conversely, with an **unsecured debt**, there is no collateral protecting the creditor. The perfect example is a credit card. When you get a new Visa card, the card issuer does not normally ask you to pledge any property as collateral to secure the debt you will incur using the card. You simply promise to pay back the debt. The debt is unsecured. Most debts that most people have—credit cards, medical bills, department store bills, and so on—are unsecured debts.

The reason why a home equity consolidation loan is a *very bad idea* is that you are trading unsecured debt for secured debt. When you stop paying an unsecured debt, there is little a creditor can do except write demand letters, make a lot of phone calls, and possibly sue you. When you stop paying a secured debt, not only do you get these same assorted tactics and threats, but—what is far worse—*you also lose the collateral that secures the debt.*

> Nancy had a home with $40,000 in equity. After her hours at work were cut back, she was having a very difficult time repaying the debt on her eight different credit cards. The total amount she owed was also $40,000. She decided to take out a second mortgage on her house at 8 percent interest (which was substantially less than the interest rate on her credit cards) and pay off all her debts. Two years later, she lost her job and was unable to continue to pay both mortgages. She lost her home in a foreclosure sale.

Had Nancy not swapped her credit card debt for a second mortgage on her house, she *would not have lost her home.* Without the new mortgage, Nancy simply could have stopped paying on the credit card debt, and earmarked any money she did make for her existing mortgage. While she undoubtedly would have received many nasty phone calls, an unsecured credit card company cannot foreclose on a house like a secured lender can. Nancy would have kept her home, and its $40,000 in equity.

Alternatively, Nancy could have declared bankruptcy, wiped out all her unsecured credit card debt, and again kept her home. Although unsecured credit card debt is discharged in bankruptcy, a secured second mortgage is not. Either alternative would have been preferable to the home equity loan.

NEGOTIATED SETTLEMENTS. A far better solution when you cannot pay your bills in full is to negotiate with your creditors and see whether any of them would be willing to accept less than full payment. This may be called a negotiated settlement, or, sometimes, a composition.

There are three aspects to settling an account for less than you owe. The first requires a compelling letter. You need to explain to your creditors that you would like to settle your account in full, but that you are simply unable to at this time. Your letter should go on to offer a settlement for an amount less than you owe. Why would a creditor accept such a proposal? Because, you explain, if it does not, you will have no choice but to declare bankruptcy, in which case, *it will get nothing*. Fifty cents on the dollar immediately starts to look like a pretty good deal.

Part two is the settlement agreement. A settlement agreement is a **contract** wherein your creditor agrees to accept, say, half of what you owe, in exchange for immediate payment of that amount in full.

That last clause, immediate payment in full, is the third part of a successful settlement. Each side must compromise something for the new contract to have legal effect; this is called **consideration**. Their compromise is reducing the amount you owe. Yours is immediate payment in full. Unless both sides compromise, the contract will have no legal effect. If you are unable to pay the compromised settlement amount in full, there is no point in using this tactic.

A typical negotiated letter and settlement may look like this:

XYZ Creditor
1800 Mariposa Ln.
Fullerton, CA
Re: Account No. 2727

Dear Customer Service:

As I have told you over the phone, I am unable to pay my

debt to you any longer. I am writing today to see whether you would be interested in settling my account.

I have consulted with a bankruptcy attorney and have learned that I could completely erase all of my debts by filing Chapter 7. *[Even if you have not met with an attorney, tell them you have. It lends credibility to your argument, and in any case, bluffing is not illegal.]* I would like to avoid that if at all possible. Therefore, I make the following offer:

1. In consideration for immediate payment of $ _____ (the "Settlement Amount"), which is 20 percent of the outstanding balance I owe your company I, _____ ("Debtor"), and your company, _____ ("Creditor"), agree to fully, completely, and forever compromise and settle this debt. *[start your offer low, at 20 percent or so, so that you can negotiate a bit higher if necessary later on.]*

2. Creditor agrees to accept the Settlement Amount as payment in full for all possible obligations Debtor may have with Creditor. *[Once your creditor accepts this offer, or something similar, this "settlement amount" is all you will owe.]* Creditor further agrees: to cease all collection activities regarding this debt; to retract all negative remarks it has reported on all of Debtor's **credit reports**; to report this debt as settled; to cease all legal proceedings against Debtor, vacate any and all **judgments** against Debtor and release any and all **garnishments** Creditor has against Debtor; and to fully release and hold harmless Debtor and his heirs or assigns from any further obligations arising from this debt. *[Essentially, you are asking them to stop all collection activities in return for payment of the settlement amount. These points are negotiable. What you really care about is settling your debt for an amount substantially less than you owe]*.

3. Within five days of receipt of a signed copy of this letter, Debtor will forward to Creditor the Settlement Amount via cashier's check or money order. This settlement will

take effect only after both parties have signed this letter and the Creditor has received the Settlement Amount. [*If you fail to pay, the settlement will be of no effect.*]

Considering the fact that I could pay you back nothing by declaring bankruptcy, I think that this settlement offer constitutes a quick and equitable solution to this problem for both parties. This offer is non-negotiable as it represents my best effort to pay you back. [*Try to negotiate as little as possible.*] If you agree to the terms of this settlement, please sign below, return this letter back to me, and I will immediately forward the Settlement Amount to you. Thank you for your consideration in this matter.

Very truly yours

Dated _____   _____
                           (Name of Debtor)

AGREED AND ACCEPTED

Dated _____   _____
                           (Name of Creditor)

                      By: _____
                           (Name and Title)

Because there are so many people filing bankruptcy these days, such settlement offers are becoming more common and more acceptable. You should hopefully expect to settle your account for about half of what you owe.

Finally, if you and a creditor cannot agree how much you owe, and you want to resolve the matter, here is a special trick that works in some parts of the country: Send the creditor a check for the amount you think you owe along with a letter explaining that you will pay nothing more. In the bottom left corner of the check, where the "memo" section is, write "P.I.F.— no recourse." "P.I.F.," as you may know, means "paid in full." "No recourse" means that the creditor can take no further actions against you for any disputed amount. The check becomes, in legal terms, an offer to settle the account. Cashing the check is an acceptance of that offer. Since offer and acceptance equals contract, if the creditor cashes your check, the matter has been settled in the amount you decided. You legally owe nothing more.

DO NOTHING. A final option is to take no action at all. If you ignore your creditors' threats, they may make a lot of annoying phone calls and threaten to sue, but there is actually not a lot they can do. (And you can easily put an immediate end to those phone calls; see chapter 3, "Dealing with Creditors and Collection Agencies.")

This is especially true if you live month-to-month and have few assets, since you are what lawyers call an "empty pocket" or "judgment proof." No creditor would waste money suing you because the likelihood of their ever getting any money back is remote. In most cases, your creditor will eventually forget about you, write off your debt as uncollectable, and get a tax break for it. Your debt might get sold to a **collection agency**, in which case the calls will begin again. After a few years (the length of time varies depending upon where you live), whoever owns your debt (actually, whoever owns the right to collect whatever you pay on the debt) will lose their right to sue, as the statute of limitations on the debt will have run out. And after seven years, the bad debt will fall off of your credit report.

As there is no such thing as debtor's prison in this country (unless you fail to pay taxes or child support), even if a creditor does sue and get a judgment, it still should not affect you, unless the creditor takes the time and effort to levy your bank account or garnish your wages (see chapter 5 "A Bankruptcy Primer"). A creditor cannot execute on a judgment by taking your furniture, clothes, or government assistance.

The Important Legal Concept to Remember: Bankruptcy is not your only option. If you have a lump sum of money, you can often settle debts for pennies on the dollar. If not, doing nothing may be the best solution. Consolidation loans are usually your worst option.

DEALING WITH CREDITORS AND COLLECTION AGENCIES

Dealing with collection agencies
What actions a creditor can legally take
How to stop all creditor harassment

DEALING WITH COLLECTION AGENCIES. A collection agency is hired by the original creditor to try and collect on your bad debt, and it is given a percentage of whatever money it gets out of you. The normal method of squeezing money out of people who do not have much is to make various threats. Consider the following example:

> Kim received a $500 loan while she attended her local business college. She never paid the loan back, and eventually the school sold the loan to ABC Collection Bureau. Thereafter, Kim started to receive daily calls from Jerry at ABC. One day, Jerry told Kim that if she did not pay at least $100 by the end of the day, he would garnish her wages. When Kim failed to pay the ransom, nothing happened.

Collection agencies just love to make hollow threats and create artificial deadlines. They tell people that if ten postdated checks are not received the next day, suit will be filed, or that if $500 is not in hand by Friday, bank accounts will be seized. But the truth is, *most of their threats are empty*, and *there is no deadline*. They make it all up. If the deadline passes, nothing happens. The threats and deadlines are nothing more than tactics used to try to pry some money out of you. Do not be intimidated.

One threat that is often made is to garnish your wages or **levy** your bank account. What is important to know is that a collection agency *cannot garnish your wages or otherwise seize your money until after it has sued you and won the suit*. Normally, it takes several months to sue someone in **small claims court** and win, and few creditors ever even bother to do this. Prior to getting a favorable court **judgment**, they cannot get any money from you unless you voluntarily send it to them.

If the threats fail to get the money, the last option available to the collection agency is in fact to sue you. This happens in surprisingly few cases. Depending upon the size of your debt, it is normally too expensive for the original creditor or the collection agency to file suit. In the case of Kim, it would likely cost ABC much more than the $500 she owes to sue. And even if it did win a judgment, what is the likelihood that ABC will ever collect? These lawsuits are usually just not cost-effective. Threats are cheaper.

Knowing that a lawsuit is unlikely, it is possible to turn the tables and demand that the debate be held on your terms.

The next time Jerry called, Kim said: "I have two things to say to you. One, I demand that you treat me with respect and speak to me like an adult. Two, I can pay you $50 a month and that is it. I will write no postdated checks. Take my $50, or sue me. That is all I can do." Jerry begrudgingly took the $50.

The key thing to remember when dealing with a collection agency is that, believe it or not, you have all of the power. You control the checkbook. If you decide not to pay, they don't get paid. If you tell them to leave you alone, they have to leave you alone. Collection agencies are nothing more than bluffing bullies of bluster.

WHAT ACTIONS A CREDITOR CAN LEGALLY TAKE. Collection agency harassment got so bad that it took congressional action to rein it in. The **Fair Debt Collections Practices Act (FDCPA)** regulates what creditors may and may not do when trying to collect a debt. The essence of the FDCPA is that debt collectors must behave in a reasonable manner and are *forbidden* from harassing the debtor. Impermissible actions may include the following:

- *Calling at the wrong place or the wrong time.* A bill collector cannot call before 8:00 A.M. or after 9:00 P.M. If so desired by the debtor, the collector *cannot call the debtor at work.*

- *Making impermissible threats.* The collection agency representative cannot use foul language, or threaten the debtor with violence, seizure of assets, or imprisonment. A threat to sue you is fine, but a threat to jail you is not (since there is no such thing as debtor's prison).

- *Using other forms of harassment.* The debt collector cannot fraudulently misrepresent who he is or what he is calling about, cannot repeatedly call the debtor, and is forbidden from publishing the debtor's name and the nature of the debt (except to a **credit bureau**).

Knowing what is acceptable creditor behavior can pay tremendous dividends. Should a creditor persist in calling you at work, tell him to stop. Should he threaten to have your car sold to pay the debt, tell him such threats are illegal. When you speak with an annoying creditor, make sure that you use the actual words "Pursuant to the Fair Debt Collections Practices Act, you cannot . . ." This lets the culprit know that you know what you are talking about.

If a collection agency continues to violate the law after being told to stop, you have two options. The first is to contact the proper authorities. The FDCPA is policed by the Federal Trade Commission. Contact the office closest to you and explain the nature of the problem. State authorities, such as your attorney general, state's attorney, or department of consumer affairs, also may investigate a serious violation of the law.

Second, the FDCPA itself permits lawsuits for violations of the Act. If violations are proven, the violator could be liable for any out-of-pocket expenses you incurred as a result of the violation, penalties up to $1,000, and possible attorneys' fees and costs. Such a suit would normally be brought in your local small claims court.

Before you undertake either action, you should first have some proof of the alleged violation. You need a tape recording of the improper threat, a copy of the illegal letter, a statement by your supervisor of an unauthorized phone call, that sort of thing. Without some evidence of the improper conduct, nothing you do will make much difference. If you cannot prove your case, you are wasting your time.

One final note about the FDCPA: while the law is a powerful tool to protect consumers, it does nothing to protect business debtors. Its application is limited solely to debts incurred for personal or family purposes.

HOW TO STOP ALL CREDITOR HARASSMENT. Maybe the best part of the FDCPA is that it allows a debtor to completely stop *all creditor phone calls*. If you have ever been subject to a pit-bull creditor who simply will not leave you alone, you do not have to be told what a relief that is. This is especially true when the creditor is slippery enough to stay within the confines of fair debt collection law, but annoying enough to make your life quite unpleasant.

Here is what you do: Write the creditor a "cease and desist" letter. This is a letter provided for in the FDCPA which tells the creditor that he is to cease and desist all further communication with you regarding this debt. The law requires that this demand be in writing; a phone call will not do. Once received, the creditor can legally contact you only *one more time*, and even then, the call can only be for the purpose of telling you how he plans to proceed (will the debt be written off, or will they file suit, that sort of thing). While a creditor retains the right to sue you, what he cannot do is write or call anymore.

Here is what your letter should look like:

ABC Collections
1800 Mariposa Ln.
Fullerton, CA
Re: Acct. 2727

Dear ABC Collections:

Pursuant to the Fair Debt Collections Practices Act, 15 U.S.C. 1592 et. seq., [*this is the specific law you are using; make sure it is in your letter just like it is written here*] you are hereby notified to cease and desist all further communication with me, and anyone associated with me, regarding the above-referenced debt. Failure to abide by this law will result in a complaint being filed against you with the Federal Trade Commission and the attorney general of my state. I also reserve the right to file suit against you for any future violations of the law.

Very truly yours,
Kim Bodian

The Important Legal Concept to Remember: The Fair Debt Collections Practices Act evened out the playing field. A debtor need not ever again accept collection agency abuse.

4

CLEANING UP YOUR
CREDIT REPORT

Understanding credit reporting
Obtaining your credit report
Correcting the report

A problem related to creditor abuse is negligent credit reporting. Some experts estimate that as many as 40 percent of all credit reports contain incorrect or outdated information. The good news is that such problems can be completely erased from your credit report. The bad news is that it takes patience and a lot of work.

UNDERSTANDING CREDIT REPORTING. As you know, probably only too well, everyone has a credit history. The "big three" companies who keep track of your bill-paying habits are Experian (formerly TRW), TransUnion, and Equifax. Each company, or credit bureau, has a file on you. When you apply for new credit, such as a car or home loan, the potential creditor will want to investigate your credit history. It does so by contacting one of these companies and buying a copy of your credit report.

Credit reports are valuable to potential creditors because they show individual financial patterns. A lone thirty-days-late notation will not hurt your chances to get that car loan; a history of continuous late payments will.

The report will include your name, Social Security number, address, history of paying bills either timely or tardily, the amount of your total indebtedness, a roster of people who have made credit inquiries about you, a list of who has and has not given you **credit**, and finally, a schedule of your current debts. Whereas credit reports used to be almost impossible to decipher, they are much simpler and more understandable today.

There is a lot of incorrect information on a lot of credit reports. The big three credit reporting agencies receive more than a billion pieces of credit information every month, and produce more than 500 million credit reports every year. The chances are quite high that there are mistakes on your report which negatively affect your financial life.

> William Johnson II had always prided himself on paying his bills on time. He was, therefore, shocked when he was turned down for a new car loan. After much investigation, it turned out that a credit reporting agency had mistakenly put his son's previous auto repossession on William's credit report. As his son still lived with him, and as his son's name was William Johnson III, the error was not hard to understand.

Besides information that does not belong to you, other common errors include:

- *Outdated information.* Other than a bankruptcy (which can legally stay on your credit report for ten years), any derogatory information can stay on your report for only seven years. If something older than that is on your report, it can and should be removed.
- *Inaccuracies.* An incorrect mark showing a thirty-days-late payment, or a mistaken tax lien, is not unheard of.
- *Lack of updates.* There are many instances where a negative

credit situation was reported to the credit agency, but your later rectification of the problem was not.

In order to rid your report of these sorts of mistakes, the first thing you will need to do is to get a copy of your report.

OBTAINING YOUR CREDIT REPORT. It is a fairly simple matter to obtain a copy of your credit report, and a smart thing to do. Not everything you think will be on it, and some things you may have forgotten about likely will be. You will also discover what you look like to potential creditors. Most importantly, negative information can be discerned and possibly deleted.

You can obtain a copy of your credit report by calling or accessing:

1. Experian
   (800) 682-7654
   www.experian.com
2. TransUnion
   (800) 851-2674
3. Equifax
   (800) 685-1111

A report normally costs about $10. Experian (which, by the way, changed its name because of the negative association many people had with the name TRW) offers all consumers one free copy of their report each year. If you have recently been denied credit, insurance, or employment because of a credit report, you can also get a free copy from any of these agencies. Pursuant to the **Fair Credit Reporting Act (FCRA)**, the credit reporting agency that issued the report causing the denial must give you a copy of your report, gratis, if you request one within thirty days of the denial.

CORRECTING THE REPORT. After reviewing your report, you may find several items that you feel are in some manner incomplete or incorrect and should not be on your credit report. If so, the FCRA permits you to challenge the entry and force the credit reporting agency to investigate and prove the item.

Here is how to challenge any item on your credit report: Write a certified letter to the agency in question (so you can verify when the letter was received) and explain in succinct terms the nature of the dispute. Give the agency your name, Social Security number, and current address. Explain the problem with the report, and attach a copy of the report to your letter.

If you can actually prove that an item is in error, all the better.

Moesha bounced a check to Larry's Hardware, and cleared up the debt a few months later. When reviewing her credit report generated by Equifax, Moesha saw that the debt was listed as unpaid. Moesha found her receipt for the payment, photocopied it, and sent it along with a letter to Equifax, demanding that the item be corrected. It was.

Any item that you dispute, even ones that you cannot prove are false, must be investigated by the credit bureau, and the bureau must then report back to you the results of its investigation. If the bureau cannot verify that its version of the disputed item is correct, then, by law, *the item must be removed from your credit report.* The standard in the industry is that the credit bureau should get back to you within thirty days. If it cannot prove the item is true within a month, then the item comes off your report.

Now, you can likely see that there is a lot of room for abuse here. Some people use this law to dispute every negative item on their report, even if they know items are correct, hoping that the credit bureau will be unable to prove the veracity of at least some of them. If a credit bureau suspects that this is your actual intent, it can legally refuse to investigate a dispute. So, here's your tip: try to challenge only those items that are disputable or unverifiable.

It may take several letters to get an item removed. If a month has gone by from the date the bureau received your initial letter and you have received no response, then write again, and demand that the item be taken off your credit report. It is critical that all correspondence be in writing so that you have a paper trail. If a bureau refuses to remove an item that you think should not be on your report any longer, then you have several options.

First, you can always go back to the original creditor and see if it will delete the item. But, unless you have paid the debt in full, removal using this method is unlikely.

Next, you can contact the proper authorities. File a complaint with your state's department of consumer affairs or attorney general, or with the Federal Trade Commission. While satisfying, this option requires time and patience in order to get the item(s) removed and your credit cleared.

Your final, and probably best, choice, is to sue. The FCRA permits lawsuits against both the original creditor and the credit bureau (whoever you think is to blame) for reporting incorrect information. If you can prove that someone is mistakenly reporting a bad debt, then file suit in small claims court. If you win, the FCRA allows you to receive money damages for your hassles. While each state is different, the most you can likely expect to see from a small claims victory is less than $5,000.

The Important Legal Concept to Remember: Credit reporting bureaus make a lot of mistakes. If an item on your report is incorrect, then it can and should be removed.

A BANKRUPTCY PRIMER

A harbor in the storm
Don't feel too bad
Bankruptcy: The ultimate trump card
Advantages and disadvantages
Types of bankruptcies
Which is best for you?

A HARBOR IN THE STORM. For many people, there comes a point where they just want to raise the white flag over their money ship and surrender. They do not want to write any more letters or explain their situation to any more nasty creditors or answer their phone anymore, not even once. Their ship is sinking.

After Richard lost his job, he had no way to take care of his family, other than using his credit cards more than he wanted. He lived off his credit cards for over a year. Once he started working again (making less than he had previously) he diligently tried to repay the $40,000 in new debt he had incurred, but fell farther and farther behind.

Richard has few options left. With debt amounts like these, no amount of fancy letter writing or negotiating is going to get him off the hook. Eventually, his creditors will sue him, win, and begin to attach his property. Once a creditor gets a judgment against a debtor, wages can be attached and applied to the amount due (a wage garnishment); bank accounts can be attached (a levy); homes can be attached (a **lien**); and property can be seized (a **seizure**).

For many people, it is divorce, uninsured medical expenses, the loss of a job, the threat of a lawsuit, or a possible wage garnishment that finally forces them to seriously consider the bankruptcy option, although far less dire circumstances can also certainly precipitate a bankruptcy. You do not have to be drowning in debt to accept the protection a bankruptcy filing affords; you merely have to be at a place where you feel you need a fresh start. Your total indebtedness could be $5,000 or $500,000—it is strictly a personal decision based upon individual circumstances (although consider that a small amount like $5,000 could be paid back and the discharge saved for a rainier day).

> Frank and Rose worked hard all their lives. As the years went by, their debts increased substantially, but they prided themselves on the fact that they always kept up with the payments. Their indebtedness was around $20,000, and they spent about $600 a month servicing that debt. Unfortunately, Rose became ill and was forced to retire. All of a sudden, bankruptcy became a viable option.

Whatever the reason, bankruptcy is a safe harbor in the financial storm, a place that can stop all creditor harassment, completely wipe out debts, and allow for a fresh start. Bankruptcy can set you free and forgive your debt. If you are at a place where it is a viable option, then forgiveness is probably a welcome, and pretty rare, sight right about now.

DON'T FEEL TOO BAD. Let's dispense with this up front: Of course you would rather pay your creditors back, if that were possible. But if you are reading this, then it may not be possible. And while you might feel bad for your creditors, it also might be helpful to know that most of them will be just fine.

Most Chapter 7 filings today result from an overaccumulation of credit card debt. The typical 20 percent interest payment that most debtors are stuck with normally results in the actual debt being paid several times over. Also, credit card issuers calculate these exorbitant interest rates, at least in part, based upon how much of the total credit they offer will likely go unpaid due to bankruptcy and defaults. One of the reasons you have been paying such a high interest rate for so long, then, is that you have been subsidizing other people's bankruptcies and defaults for many years. And in any case, your credit card companies will just have to get by without your monthly payment and will have to live with the tax write-off they will receive. That is one of the costs of capitalism. Do not fret. Your creditors will survive.

Understand too that bankruptcy is a statutory right that has been part of civilized societies for thousands of years. Corporations file for bankruptcy protection all the time. Like you, sometimes they need help. In the past few years, over one million Americans a year have sought bankruptcy protection. So feel bad if you must, but get over it. You are in good company. Yes, you should learn your lessons and not get in this mess again. But both bankruptcy and this country are about second chances. If you need to, take yours.

BANKRUPTCY: THE ULTIMATE TRUMP CARD. The whole point of bankruptcy is to give cash-strapped, scared, harried, overextended, well-intentioned debtors a chance to start over without any more creditor harassment. It does so in many ways.

The very first thing to happen that will make your life easier occurs the moment you **file** your bankruptcy paperwork, when the **bankruptcy court** issues an order, called the **automatic stay**. The stay is a federal court order that *immediately puts a halt to all collection activities*. It is not called an *automatic* stay for nothing—the stay is ordered immediately upon the filing of every bankruptcy.

The breadth of the stay is impressive indeed.

SDS Collection Bureau had been hounding Jill for several months. Finally, it filed suit against her in small claims court. The day before she was set to go to trial, Jill filed a Chapter 7 bankruptcy. The next day Jill showed up in court, showed the clerk her bankruptcy paperwork, and the trial was canceled.

The stay stops *all collector actions* dead in their tracks. It stops lawsuits. It stops wage garnishments. It stops all phone calls and letters. It stops auto repossessions. It even stops home foreclosures. Now, think about that for a minute. Your home could be on the block, ready to be sold at a foreclosure sale tomorrow, and if you file bankruptcy today, the sale will be stopped. No matter what action a collector is about to take against you, you hold the ultimate trump card: bankruptcy and the automatic stay.

The automatic stay remains in effect for the duration of the bankruptcy, usually about four months for a Chapter 7. At the end of the case, the debtor receives a discharge, another court order stating that the debts have been forgiven and the debtor is no longer liable for them.

Thus, for most people, the filing of the case and the corresponding issuance of the automatic stay means that they will never have to deal with most of their creditors again. The stay stops all communication during the course of the bankruptcy proceedings, and the discharge forgives the debts altogether.

ADVANTAGES AND DISADVANTAGES. The automatic stay is the first of many advantages that a bankruptcy filing affords a weary debtor. The other obvious benefit is that most, if not all, of your debts will be completely wiped out when the case ends and you receive your discharge. You could owe $80,000 to six different credit cards, and the entire debt will be forgiven at the conclusion of your case.

This in turn has another, tangential, benefit.

Wendy was having $200 of her paycheck garnished every month by one of her creditors. She then filed for Chapter 7 bankruptcy. The garnishment was released. On top of that, she no longer had to pay the other $600 that she had been paying on her other debts every month. All of a sudden, Wendy had an extra $800 a month that she did not have before filing.

For Wendy, filing bankruptcy was almost like getting a raise. The opportunity to get rid of $800 a month in payments freed up a lot of disposable income for her, money she could use for more essential needs.

One final advantage to filing bankruptcy is the peace of mind it creates for many people. Few problems cause more marital strife and personal stress than financial ones. Bankruptcy, with its chance to start anew and get creditors off your back, will help you get along better with your mate and enable you to sleep better at night.

Of course there are downsides to filing bankruptcy. These are the most notable:

· *The effect on your credit report.* Unlike other types of credit notations, which stay on your credit report for seven years, a bankruptcy stays on for ten years.

· *The effect on future credit.* Filing bankruptcy does not mean that you will never get credit again. It does mean that the credit you do get will be more expensive. Whereas you might be able to get a car loan at 10 percent today, that same loan will cost around 20 percent after you **file**. While people routinely get home loans about two years after their bankruptcy is concluded, they pay higher interest, and are charged more points, to get that loan. Credit cards will be secured rather than unsecured for the foreseeable future.

- *Loss of property*. In a small number of cases, a person may lose some of her property to the bankruptcy **trustee**. This only occurs when the person files her bankruptcy without assistance of counsel (called filing **pro per**) and does not know what she is doing, or has a bad attorney, or owns too much property. (See chapter 7, "Protecting Your Personal Property.")

- *Stigma*. While there used to be a great stigma about filing bankruptcy, that is far less true today. With so many people doing it, and so many notable businesses and celebrities doing it, for good or ill, there is not much social stigma left.

Although there are certainly some negative aspects to filing bankruptcy, the truth is, for most people who are at a point where they are seriously contemplating it, the benefits usually outweigh the burdens.

TYPES OF BANKRUPTCIES. There are four types of bankruptcies individuals may consider: Chapter 7, Chapter 11, Chapter 12, and Chapter 13 (these are chapters of the United States Bankruptcy Code). As already noted, Chapter 7 is by far the most common one used by consumers, and is usually the best choice. Chapter 11 is used by large businesses who want to reorganize their debts, and sometimes by very wealthy individuals. It is inappropriate to almost all consumer debtors. Chapter 12 is a type of bankruptcy specifically designed to help family farmers. Its use too is fairly rare. Like Chapter 11, Chapter 13 is also a type of **reorganization** of debt, but is intended for use by consumers. In a small number of cases, the use of a Chapter 13 makes sense. Almost all consumers or small businesses will file either a Chapter 7 or a Chapter 13 bankruptcy.

WHICH IS BEST FOR YOU? You want to, and most likely will, file a Chapter 7 bankruptcy. A Chapter 13 is used only in *very specific, limited circumstances*. It is most often used to save a home that is about to be foreclosed upon.

Marla and Stuart were having a difficult time keeping up with their mortgage and bills. They were two months behind on their house payment when their lender started foreclosure proceedings. They consulted with an attorney and filed Chapter 13. By doing so, they were able to repay their past-due mortgage over a three-year period to the bankruptcy trustee, who, in turn, repaid their lender.

The heart of a Chapter 13 is a repayment **plan** that lasts anywhere from three to five years, depending on the circumstances. The debtor promises to pay a certain amount of money each month to the Chapter 13 trustee, who in turn pays back the debtor's creditors. Typically, secured debtors are repaid 100 percent, and unsecured creditors get back only a portion of what they are owed.

Besides making up home mortgage **arrears**, the only other time a Chapter 13 is normally used is when a debtor has **nonexempt assets**. Each state has a different set of rules, called **exemptions**, which are used to determine how much property a debtor can keep in a Chapter 7. Essentially, exemption means protection. If you are able to exempt property, that means you are able to protect it and keep it. Although the exemption rules in some states are generous, they are not limitless. If the value of your property is more than the exemption rules of your state allow, and you file a Chapter 7, the trustee in your case will take and sell whatever property you own that is over the limit. Another reason a Chapter 13 is used is to avoid that possibility.

It took thirty years, but Shirley finally paid off her mortgage. Her home was worth $75,000. In her state, the exemption limit on home equity was $50,000. If Shirley filed a Chapter 7, her bankruptcy trustee would take her house, sell it, pay Shirley the $50,000 she was legally permitted to exempt, and use the other $25,000 to pay her creditors. If she filed a Chapter 13, Shirley could keep her home.

Another reason that a person may choose a Chapter 13 is that it allows for what is called a "super-discharge." As discussed in more detail in chapter 6, "Do You Have the Right Type of Debts?," not all debts are discharged by a Chapter 7 bankruptcy; for example, debts induced by fraud. A Chapter 13 super-discharge allows for discharge of these sorts of debts whereas a Chapter 7 does not.

Normally, however, a Chapter 7 is almost always a better choice. It is much simpler than a Chapter 13—there is no plan and no ongoing payments to the trustee. It is quick—about four months from start to finish, as opposed to a minimum of three years for a Chapter 13 case. Chapter 7s cost less—legal fees are considerably lower in a Chapter 7 than in a Chapter 13. Best of all, it solves the problem—debtors normally pay nothing back to their creditors.

The reason that a Chapter 7 makes sense for most consumer debtors is that they have a lot of unsecured debt—credit cards, medical bills, lines of credit, that sort of thing. Whereas a Chapter 13 forces a debtor to repay some of this money over a several-year period, a Chapter 7 completely avoids that. Not a penny is paid back to unsecured creditors in a Chapter 7.

It is also attractive because most states create exemption limits high enough to allow most debtors to keep all of their property. It is this chance to discharge all debts and keep all property that makes Chapter 7 so appealing. Taking into consideration its relatively short duration as well, a Chapter 7 is far more preferable than a Chapter 13.

If you have a lot of unsecured debt, or a mix of secured and unsecured, then Chapter 7 makes sense. If you are about to lose a home or car to a bank, or have a lot of non-exempt property, then a Chapter 13 is your best bet.

The Important Legal Concept to Remember: Bankruptcy affords you the chance to get rid of creditors and old debts and get a start fresh. If at all possible, file a Chapter 7.

II

CHAPTER 7
PRE-FILING
CONSIDERATIONS

DO YOU HAVE THE RIGHT TYPE OF DEBTS?

Types of debts
Secured debts
Options for secured debts
Unsecured debts
Student loans and taxes
Nondischargeable debts

TYPES OF DEBTS. The first thing to consider when contemplating a bankruptcy is whether you have the sorts of debts that will be discharged by filing a Chapter 7. There are many different types of debts that a person can have, and not all are wiped out by a bankruptcy. If you have a lot of debts that will not be wiped out in a Chapter 7, there is no point in filing this type of bankruptcy.

Most people have two main types of debts: secured and unsecured debts. There are also other types of debts that don't fall into these categories, such as taxes, student loans, child support, and alimony. The important thing to figure out is whether a bankruptcy will get rid of your particular debts, or at least enough of your debts to make a difference.

SECURED DEBTS. Again, a secured debt is one that is attached to some sort of collateral.

Jon really needed a new car, so he went to the bank to see if he could obtain financing. He was told that the bank would lend him $10,000 to buy the new car, but would keep title to the car until the loan was paid off. Jon agreed to the terms of the loan and borrowed the $10,000. Jon's debt is secured.

In Jon's case, the bank agreed to lend him the money to buy the car, but would do so only if the debt was secured by some collateral, namely, the car Jon wanted to buy. If Jon fails to pay back the loan, the bank will repossess the car and sell it to pay back the loan. The car secures the loan.

Besides car loans, home loans are also secured. The bank lends you the money to buy your home but keeps a mortgage against it. If you do not pay back the loan, the bank forecloses, sells your house, and gets paid back.

There are many other sorts of secured debts:

- *Judgment liens.* When someone sues you and wins, that is called getting a judgment. The holder of a judgment can file a lien against the property of the one who owes the judgment. That is called a **judgment lien.** When the property is sold (usually a house or car) the lein is paid.

- *Second and third mortgages.* Any time you use equity in your home to get a loan, a mortgage is created. All mortgages are secured debts.

- *Items bought at department stores.* Creditors such as Sears and J. C. Penny, as well as most electronics stores, have, surely unbeknownst to you, a security agreement as part of their standard credit application. That means that many of the expensive items you buy at these places through the use of their credit cards are secured items. If you bought a refrigerator last year at Sears with your Sears card, that is a secured debt. Surprise, surprise.

- *Finance company loans.* Loans made against household goods by finance companies (such as AVCO and Household Finance Co.) are also secured debts.

The important thing to understand is that secured debts are not automatically discharged in a bankruptcy. Although your *personal liability* for the debt will be discharged, the *security interest* survives the bankruptcy. This is a very important, and equally difficult, concept to grasp.

A secured creditor essentially has two means to collect its money if its debt is not repaid. The first is simply to take back the property securing the debt—the car is repossessed, the house is foreclosed upon. But if the resale of the property repossessed is not enough to cover the debt, the lender can always use the second method to get paid in full—the personal liability of the debtor for the debt.

Cordell still owed $10,000 on his car loan when it became impossible for him to continue the car payments. After Cordell fell three months behind on the payment, his bank repossessed his car. The bank sold the car at a wholesale auction for $6,000, and then sued Cordell for the other $4,000.

It is Cordell's personal liability that allows the bank to sue him for the difference (called the **deficiency balance**). In a bankruptcy, that second method of repayment, the personal liability for the debt, is discharged. But the first method of repayment, the security interest, survives the bankruptcy. This means that, after a bankruptcy, the only recourse a lender holding a security interest has is to take the property back. It cannot sue the debtor for any deficiency balance.

It should make sense, then, that when you have a secured debt going into a bankruptcy, you will still have to repay at least the **fair market value** of the property if you want to keep it. If you do not repay the secured lender at least the value of the secured property, the lender can and will take the property back after the bankruptcy.

OPTIONS FOR SECURED DEBTS. Accordingly, with most secured debts, you have four options when you file for bankruptcy. Three of those options relate to keeping the debt. The fourth is a way to get rid of the debt.

> A year after Jon bought his new car, he lost his job. Unable to keep up with his debts any longer, Jon decided to declare bankruptcy. His main concern was that he really wanted to keep his car. He knew that he would be getting a new job eventually, and that if he was able to get rid of his large credit card debt, he would be able to still make his car payments.

Jon can keep his car if he wants to. When a person files for bankruptcy, part of the paperwork is a page called the **statement of intention**. In it, the debtor states his intent with regard to his secured merchandise. A debtor who wants to keep a secured debt, can state on his statement of intention that he will do one of the following:

1. *Reaffirm the debt.* A **reaffirmation** is an agreement between the debtor and the creditor stating that the debtor desires to keep the property, agrees to keep paying for it, and *agrees to remain personally liable for the debt.* In essence, the debtor and the creditor enter into a new contract by signing the reaffirmation. Because a debtor is reestablishing personal liability, reaffirmations *are not recommended* if they can be avoided. (For more information, see chapter 12, "How the Case Proceeds.")

2. *Redeem the debt.* A **redemption** is also a new contract between the debtor and the creditor. Whereas a reaffirmation is a contract to pay back the debt in monthly installments, a redemption is a contract to pay back the debt in a reduced lump sum. Because no new personal liability is being created, a redemption is preferred over a reaffirmation. Sears

might agree to let you keep that refrigerator if you agree to pay $250 within thirty days.

3. *Retain the debt.* In some states, not all, a debtor can simply keep paying the debt without entering into a new contract. This is called **retention**. This is very advantageous for the debtor because no new personal liability is being established, as with a reaffirmation agreement, and no lump-sum payment is required, as with a redemption. Retention usually occurs with car loans and mortgages where the debtor continues to make scheduled payments throughout the bankruptcy proceedings.

Aside from these three options, a debtor can also get rid of the debt, as long as he is willing to **surrender** the property.

Right before he filed, Jon decided that he really could not afford the payments on his car anymore. In his statement of intention, he declared that it was his desire to surrender his car back to the lender.

The surrender option is very powerful. If you own a car in which you are "upside down" (you owe far more than the car is worth), you can surrender the car back to the lender during your bankruptcy, get out of the contract, and owe nothing more on the vehicle. The secured merchandise is returned, and your personal liability will be discharged. Nothing more will be owed.

Now, if you simply could not keep up with your payments and did not declare bankruptcy, your lender would eventually repossess the car and sue you for the difference between what it sold the car for and what you owe, called the deficiency balance. By surrendering it in your bankruptcy, you completely wipe out any obligation you have for the vehicle. If your house is worth far less than you owe on it, you can surrender it back to your lender. This option to surrender is quite amazing, as *there is no other area of law that allows you to unilaterally get out of a bad contract.*

The bottom line is that it is only your personal liability, but not the entire secured debt, that is normally discharged in your bankruptcy. If most of your debts are secured, Chapter 7 bankruptcy may not solve your problems, although the option to get out of a bad contract still makes it attractive to some people.

UNSECURED DEBTS. Unsecured debts are not associated with any sort of collateral. The typical example is a credit card. When a credit card company issues you a credit card, it normally does not ask for any sort of collateral. The card is unsecured, and whatever you buy with it is also unsecured. Most debts that most people have are unsecured. Besides credit cards, other types of unsecured debts are:

· Medical bills

· Legal bills

· Utility bills

· Unsecured lines of credit

· Bounced checks

· Miscellaneous purchases

The great thing about unsecured debts insofar as bankruptcy is concerned is that these debts are *completely wiped out by a Chapter 7 bankruptcy.* This means, for example, that you could owe $100,000 on eight different credit cards, $5,000 in medical bills, and another $2,000 in other bills, and have this amount discharged entirely in your bankruptcy. In a Chapter 7, there is no limit as to how much unsecured debt you can have discharged (which is not true for a Chapter 13). In most cases, the only time an unsecured debt will not be discharged is if some type of **fraud** is involved. (See chapter 13, "What Can Go Wrong?")

If you are having a difficult time figuring out whether a certain debt you have is secured or unsecured, the key question to ask yourself is this: have you pledged any sort of collateral to secure the debt, or is there some sort of lien (judgment lien, mechanic's lien, tax lien) associated with the debt? If the answer is no, then the debt is unsecured. Most debt that most people have is unsecured debt.

If you have a lot of unsecured debts, then filing Chapter 7 makes sense. Unsecured debts are the easiest type of debts to get discharged in a bankruptcy.

STUDENT LOANS AND TAXES. Secured and unsecured debts are useful categorizations for most debts. But most debts are not all debts. There are other sorts of debts that you may have that do not fall within those categories. Two other, common, sorts of debts are student loans and taxes. Are they dischargeable? Maybe.

Student loans are not normally dischargeable, although there are two ways to get them discharged. The first method necessitates waiting the requisite number of years before filing your case. If the date that your loan finally came due, excluding all forbearances and deferments, is more than seven years before the date you file bankruptcy, then your student loan is dischargeable. For example, if payments on your student loan came due March 1, 1991, then they would become dischargable if you filed your bankruptcy at least seven years later, on or after March 2, 1998.

When Jon filed his bankruptcy in 1996, he listed his student loans, anticipating that they would be discharged, since they came due in 1989. What he forgot was that he had asked for, and received, a deferment for a year, in 1992. Because a full seven years had not elapsed (the deferment shortened it by a year), the student loans were not discharged.

Although bankruptcy is federal law (meaning that it applies to all states equally), each federal appellate jurisdiction interprets bankruptcy law differently. Accordingly, different areas of the country apply this seven-year test differently. If you are filing bankruptcy in order to discharge a student loan, it is imperative that you speak with a bankruptcy attorney to make sure that your situation fits the guidelines in your area.

The other way to get rid of a student loan in bankruptcy is to pass the "undue hardship" test. The tripartite test is:

1. The debtor cannot maintain even a minimal standard of living if forced to repay the loan;
2. This state of affairs is likely to exist for a significant portion of the repayment period; and
3. The debtor has made good faith efforts to repay the loan.

Note that all three parts of the test must be met to qualify for a hardship discharge and there are large regional variations as to how this test is applied. If you think you qualify for a hardship discharge, you will need to bring a **motion** before your bankruptcy judge and get a judicial determination to that effect. Unless you are almost destitute, do not waste your time and money trying to get student loans discharged this way.

Taxes too are not easily discharged. Are you surprised? While there are simply too many kinds of taxes for any sort of detail here, essentially, taxes are dischargeable if

1. a tax return for the year in question was filed on time, or if not, then at least two years before the bankruptcy;
2. the tax is over three years old;
3. the tax was assessed more than 240 days before the bankruptcy is filed; and
4. the debtor did not willfully evade the taxes.

If this does not apply to you, it still may be possible to get rid of the debt in a Chapter 13 bankruptcy. (See chapter 14, "Chapter 13 Made Easy.")

If you are filing bankruptcy to get rid of student loans or taxes, exercise extreme caution. These debts are not easily discharged.

NONDISCHARGEABLE DEBTS. Finally, certain types of debts are considered **nondischargeable**. These debts are never discharged in a Chapter 7. No questions, no debate, no motions, nothing. Those debts are:

1. Taxes which do not pass the above-stated requirements.
2. Debts that were not listed on the bankruptcy. Any debt not listed will not be discharged.
3. Alimony and child support obligations.
4. Government fines and penalties.
5. Student loans which do not pass the above-stated test.
6. Debts arising from drunk driving or illegal drug use.
7. Debts that were denied or waived in a prior bankruptcy.
8. Debts incurred to pay nondischargeable taxes (e.g., you used a credit card to pay your taxes.)
9. Debts for various condominium and cooperative assessments.
10. Debts incurred by defrauding a bank.
11. Debts imposed by courts upon prisoners filing lawsuits.

The following four categories of debts are also nondischargeable, *but only if the creditor files a **complaint** with the bankruptcy court and gets a judge to **order** that they are not dischargeable*. If that does not occur in your bankruptcy, and you list these sorts of debts, they would be discharged along with the rest of your dischargeable debts if no one complains.

1. *Debts incurred through false pretenses.* For most consumers, this would relate to an excessive use of their credit cards right before filing bankruptcy.
2. *Debts resulting from fraud.* Debts incurred because of stealing or embezzling money are not normally dischargeable.

Similarly, a fiduciary (such as a trustee of a trust) cannot commit fraud and get the debt discharged without argument.

3. *Debts resulting from willful or malicious injury.* For example, you cannot get rid of a debt incurred because you intentionally punched someone.

4. *An unpaid property settlement arising from a divorce.* Although alimony and child support are flatly nondischargeable, an unpaid property settlement is not so automatic. (For more information, see the companion book, *Ask a Lawyer: Divorce and Child Custody.*)

All fifteen of these so-called "exceptions to discharge" are complicated. Again, an expert is probably needed to help you determine whether any apply to you.

The bad news is that if any of the exceptions in the first list apply to you, the debt would not be discharged in your bankruptcy. The good news is that if any of the debts in the second list apply to you, the debt would be discharged unless the negatively affected party complains and wins.

The Important Legal Concept to Remember: Most people have a lot of unsecured debt, and for them, a Chapter 7 bankruptcy would surely make their life easier since those debts are easily discharged. Other debts are more difficult to get rid of.

PROTECTING YOUR PERSONAL PROPERTY

Assets of the estate
Exemption rules in general
What property is exempt?
Valuing your property
If you are over the limit

Aside from figuring out whether your debts are dischargeable, the other major consideration before filing bankruptcy relates to property. One of the greatest fears people have about bankruptcy is that they will lose their property if they file. While understandable, this is mostly a misconception.

The entire purpose of bankruptcy is to give those people who need it a fresh start. Very few people would ever file if it meant that they would lose their homes or cars. You could not really get a fresh start if that were to happen, could you? Accordingly, bankruptcy laws in most states are actually quite generous with regard to property. Most—not all, mind you, but most—consumer debtors are able to keep all of their property throughout their bankruptcy.

ASSETS OF THE ESTATE. When you fill out your bankruptcy paperwork (called your **petition** and **schedules**), one of the first things you will need to do is to list all of your assets, both

real property and **personal property**. Collectively, everything you own at the time you file comprises what is called your **bankruptcy estate**.

The contents of your estate include all of the following:

1. *Property in your possession.* This would include all furniture, household goods and items, cars, and so on.

2. *Property you own but not in your possession.* Things like security deposits held by landlords and utility companies, or televisions on loan to a brother, are also yours and part of your estate. In addition, and importantly, if you are filing around tax time, any tax refund you are due is considered part of your estate. *Make sure to list it and exempt it (see below) so that you can keep it.*

3. *Real estate.* Aside from your house, this would also include time-share condos, rental property, realty in other states, and unimproved lots.

4. *Pension and trust income.* If you are entitled to future income from a pension, such as a 401(k), or an IRA, this too must be listed. Similarly, if you are currently a beneficiary of a will, trust, or estate (meaning you are now receiving money from one of those sources), then this is also an item to be included as part of your bankruptcy estate.

Needless to say, your bankruptcy estate is quite expansive. It consists of everything you conceivably own. While you might be tempted to "forget" to list an asset, or give one away right before filing, don't. You are required, under penalty of perjury, a $500,000 fine, and possible jail time, to list *everything that you own*. If you own only part of something, such as property held in joint tenancy or as community property, then you are required to list only your proportional share of that property.

EXEMPTION RULES IN GENERAL. In order to keep everything you conceivably own (your estate), it all must be exempted.

When you exempt a piece of property, you are telling the bankruptcy court that you plan to keep that property. The actual process of exempting property consists of nothing more than listing all property you own in your schedules and then listing the corresponding laws that allow you to keep that property.

While the exemption process may seem simple, it actually is not, because each state puts different limits on how much property a debtor can keep when he files for bankruptcy. Some states, like Florida, for example, are exceptionally liberal with their exemption laws. Others are not.

> Mike and Ethel were an elderly couple who lived in Georgia. They had a home which they owned outright, worth $200,000, and $100,000 in unsecured debts. Because they wanted to live out their few remaining years comfortably, they decided to get their debts discharged in bankruptcy. The problem was, Georgia only allows a couple to protect $5,000 equity in a home. If Mike and Ethel filed in Georgia, they would lose their house in the bankruptcy. They decided instead to retire next door to Florida, where homes are completely protected, no matter what they are worth.

In New York, a single person can only exempt $10,000 worth of equity in a home, and a married couple, $20,000. In Delaware, there is no **homestead exemption** at all.

The reason why exemptions are probably *the most critical element* to your bankruptcy is that when you file your paperwork, a bankruptcy trustee is appointed by the court to review your case and the assets of your estate. *If you do not exempt your assets, or if your property is worth more than your state's exemptions allow, the trustee will take your non-exempt belongings, sell them, and use the money to pay back your creditors.*

WHAT PROPERTY IS EXEMPT? Some states allow debtors to choose from either their own state exemption system or the federal exemption system. Most states, however, have only one exemption system and no choice. What you want to figure out is whether your state's system(s) would allow you to exempt all of your assets.[1]

The federal exemption system is mimicked by many of the states, and is therefore useful to explain what is actually protectable. The following items are exempt under the federal exemption rules.

PROPERTY PROTECTED	AMOUNT PROTECTED
1. Homestead (homes)	$15,000 equity if single; $30,000 equity if married
2. Automobiles	$2,400 equity per car; only one car allowed per person
3. Household goods	$400 in any individual item
4. Jewelry	$1,000 total
5. Tools of the trade	$1,500
6. Health aids	Unlimited, if professionally prescribed
7. Pensions	**ERISA** qualified pensions totally exempt
8. Personal injury recoveries	$15,000
9. Wild card	$800 per debtor, plus any *unused portion of the homestead*, up to $7,500 per debtor. Total possible: $8,300 per debtor ($7,500 + $800)

While your state will, in all likelihood, have a different list with different amounts,[2] the bulk of it will look something similar to this one.

The important thing about an exemption system is that it is the equity in, not the **gross value** of, your property that is the critical factor.

1. At the time this book is being prepared (September, 1997), Congress is considering making changes to federal bankruptcy laws. One of the main areas of review concerns state exemption rules, and one of the main areas of possible alteration is the creation of a mandatory, uniform federal bankruptcy exemption system. Make sure to check with an expert in your area regarding exemption rules and any other possible recent changes to bankruptcy laws.

2. This system is used only by Arkansas, Connecticut, the District of Columbia, Hawaii, Massachusetts, Michigan, Minnesota, New Jersey, New Mexico, Pennsylvania, Rhode Island, South Carolina, Texas, Vermont, Washington, and Wisconsin.

Milton has a home worth $100,000 with a $75,000 mortgage. Milton has only $25,000 worth of equity in his home,
and thus needs to exempt *only that amount*. He also owes
$9,000 on a car that is worth $10,000. Milton needs to
exempt only the $1,000 equity he has in the car in order to
keep it.

Remember, it is just the equity in your property that you
need to exempt.

The next thing to understand about exempting property is
how the last item in this list, the **wild card**, works. In most
cases, *it is the wild card that will allow you to keep your personal
property.*

Initially, the thing to realize about the wild card is that it
can only be used if you do not have a house, or at least not
much equity in one. The wild card cannot be used to protect
both a lot of home equity *and* personal property, since the wild
card is primarily based upon *the unused portion of your homestead exemption* (save for $800; see item 9 in federal exemptions
above). If you use your homestead exemption to protect the
equity in your home, then there will be no unused portion for
your wild card.

It helps to think of the homestead exemption as gasoline.
You are allotted $7,500 worth of homestead gas and $800 in
wild card gas. If you use all of your homestead fuel exempting
your house, then you have none left over to further fuel your
wild card. If you do not own a home, then you can siphon all of
your homestead gas to fuel your wild card exemption. If you
are married, you can double these numbers.

Sumi's home is worth $100,000 and she owes $100,000 on
it. Since she has no equity in her house, she does not need to
use her homestead exemption gasoline to protect her house
(you only need to exempt *equity*). She can combine her
$7,500 worth of unused homestead fuel and her $800 wild
card fuel ($8,300 total) and use it all as wild card exemp-
tion to protect other property.

Bill's home is also worth $100,000, and he owes $90,000. He would need to use $10,000 of his homestead fuel to protect his home equity. The remaining $5,000 of homestead gas could be combined with his $800 wild card gas, and he could use all $5,800 as wild card fuel to protect other property.

Larry and Susan have $30,000 worth of equity in their home. They would have to use all of their homestead exemption fuel to protect their house and would have only $800 to use as wild card protection.

Chris does not own a home. Since he has no need for a homestead exemption, he has $7,500 of homestead fuel and $800 wild card fuel ($8,300 total) to use on other property.

The other important thing about the wild card, once it has been gassed up, is that it can be used to protect a single item, or multiple items, up to the wild card exemption limit.

Jacob owns no home but has a fishing boat worth $5,000, and $1,000 in the bank. Although the federal system does not have exemptions that would specifically protect these items, Jacob can use the wild card to protect them. In fact, since the federal wild card ceiling is $8,300, and his boat and money combined only total $6,000, Jacob would still have $2,300 in wild card exemption room left to protect other property

The wild card is a great tool that allows many debtors to keep most, if not all, of their property. For example, under the federal system, household goods can only be protected up to a value of $400 per item. If you own a large-screen television worth $1,500, the wild card can be used to protect that. You would combine $400 from your household goods exemption with $1,100 from your wild card exemption, totaling $1,500, and keep the TV. If it were Jacob who owned the television, even then he would still have $1,200 of wild card exemption room to protect other valuable items.

Because each state is different and allows exemptions and wild cards in different amounts, and because these rules may change in the future, you *are strongly advised to seek out a bankruptcy attorney to draft your bankruptcy paperwork*, if for no other reason than to make sure that your property is protected. If you do it wrong, you could end up losing, literally, the shirt off your back.

VALUING YOUR PROPERTY. There are other ways to protect your property besides (or in addition to) using the wild card. The first is to value your property as low as possible in your bankruptcy paperwork. Going through bankruptcy is a little bit like going through the looking glass; everything is kind of upside down. In real life, it is not great to have too many debts, but in bankruptcy, it does not really matter since they will be discharged anyway. In real life, you want to have valuable property, but in bankruptcy, you want to be able to show that your property is not worth a whole lot. That way, your property would fit under your state's exemption ceiling and be protected.

Remember, if your property is over the limit, the trustee overseeing your case has the right to take it and sell it. He will keep part of the proceeds and use the bulk of the money to pay your creditors. You *must* get your property below the exemption limits allowed by your state.

You do so by listing the *lowest possible, albeit ostensibly reasonable, value for your assets.* When valuing your car, use the low blue book instead of the high blue book. Even better, use the price listed in the classified ads, as that is generally lower then even the low blue book. Make sure to reduce its value even more for high mileage, problems in need of repair, that sort of thing.

If that price still puts you over the exemption limit, try this dandy trick: Take your car to a used car lot and ask them what you could get for it on a trade-in. That will be the rock bottom price. Have the dealership write it on the back of their business card, and attach it to your bankruptcy schedules. They might charge you $50, but it also might save your car.

What you are trying to do is reduce the amount of equity you show in a piece of property that is potentially over the limit. Although your refrigerator may have cost $1,000 new, what would it be worth at a garage sale today? $100? $200? Using the yard sale or liquidation value for your property in your schedules is perfectly acceptable and intelligent.

Finally, there is one more thing to consider. If you simply cannot get a particular piece of property under the limit, you need to ask yourself whether the trustee really would bother taking it and selling it. An old aluminum fishing boat worth $200 (for the sake of argument, non-exempt) still may be of no interest to the trustee. How much would it cost him to get it and sell it? Who could he sell it to? How much time would it take? Similarly, it is very doubtful that a trustee would sell a home that is, say $1,000 over the exemption limit.

If all of this seems complicated, that is because it is. An attorney is really needed to make sure your assets are properly protected.

IF YOU ARE OVER THE LIMIT. What happens if you have a piece of property that you simply cannot exempt and is actually worth something to the trustee? You may or may not lose it.

> Maria owned a car that had $5,000 in equity. The exemption laws of her state allowed her to protect only $2,400. After she filed bankruptcy, the trustee in her case took the car and sold it. He paid Maria $2,400, because she exempted that amount, and used the other $2,600 to partially pay back her creditors.

The rule is, any property which is not exempt can be taken and sold by the trustee. He is required to pay you the amount you are able to exempt. He would use the rest of the money to satisfy creditor **claims**.

Francesco's car was $5,000 over the exemption limit, and he wanted to keep it. After the trustee took the car, but before she sold it, Francesco called her and offered to pay her what she would have received if she had sold it—$5,000. The trustee agreed, and Francesco borrowed the money from his pal Jeff, paid the trustee, and kept the car.

Most trustees are pretty easy to work with. Trustees are hired and professionally trained by the local United States trustee's office. If you have an asset that is worth more than the exemption limit, you will likely find your trustee is more than willing to work out a payment arrangement and allow you to keep the property, if you so choose. It saves her the time and effort of having to sell the merchandise.

The Important Legal Concept to Remember: Property not exempted is property lost. With a dose of creativity, you should be able to protect all of your property (depending upon your state's laws). To be safe, expert help should be employed.

8

PROTECTING YOUR HOUSE

Your mortgage and bankruptcy
Exempting your house
If you are over the limit

While most people have a general fear that they may lose some unspecified property if they file bankruptcy, homeowners have a very specific fear that they will lose their home. Whether they will be able to keep their house depends upon two factors: the state of their mortgage and their state's exemptions rules.

YOUR MORTGAGE AND BANKRUPTCY. Insofar as your mortgage goes, if you are current on your mortgage payments, then there will be no reason for your lender to attempt to take your house if you file for bankruptcy.

As with any other secured debt you plan on keeping, you will need to continue to make your scheduled monthly mortgage payments throughout your bankruptcy. Although you are required to list your lender as a secured creditor, as long as you are current, the bankruptcy will have no effect on your mortgage. Your lender will not suddenly foreclose because you file for bankruptcy; your loan and your payments will remain exactly the same. When your case is over, you will continue to make payments as if nothing has happened.

Things are a bit different if you are behind on your mortgage and you want to file a Chapter 7. In that case, you will need to make up the past-due amount within about a month or two from the date you file, *as well as* keeping current throughout the entire case. If you remain in arrears after filing bankruptcy, your lender will eventually go before the bankruptcy court and ask for permission to foreclose on your house. Your lender needs to ask for permission to do this because the automatic stay remains in effect until your case is over, and no creditor can proceed with any action against you, outside of bankruptcy court, without court approval. (See also chapter 13, "What Can Go Wrong?")

If you are behind, you need to get caught up as soon as possible. Hopefully, after filing, you will have a bit more discretionary income. Use it and get current on your home.

If you do not see any way to get current, then your other option would be to file a Chapter 13 bankruptcy. The only way to get rid of mortgage arrears in a bankruptcy is to pay them off through a Chapter 13 plan, and you would have three years to do it.

EXEMPTING YOUR HOUSE. Appendix C lists the different homestead exemption amounts allowed by each state. As you can see, the exemption amount available varies greatly from state to state. Pennsylvania has no homestead exemption, and Minnesota's is unlimited. Again, it is equity, not gross value, that determines the amount you need to exempt.

To figure out whether you will be able to fully exempt your house, you will need to do two things:

1. Figure out how much equity is actually in your home. Look at comparable home sales in your neighborhood to get a good idea of what your house would be worth if you were to sell it today. Subtract the amount you owe your lender(s), and that is your equity.

2. Look up the equity limits in Appendix C and see if you fall under the limit for your state.

IF YOU ARE OVER THE LIMIT. As in the previous chapter, you want to show in your paperwork the lowest possible, yet nevertheless reasonable, amount of equity in your home, so that you fall under your state's exemption limit.

The first thing to do is to value your home at the lowest reasonable amount.

Sam's home was possibly worth as much as $225,000, which would show him having $75,000 in equity. The exemption limit in his state is $40,000. To reduce his equity, the first thing Sam did before filing was to have a friend who was a realtor get the numbers on several recent comparable home sales in Sam's neighborhood. It turned out that several homes, not quite as nice as Sam's, but similar, had sold for around $200,000. Sam used that amount as the value of his home in his schedules.

By doing just a bit of homework, Sam was able to reduce the value of his house by $25,000. Remember, you are through the looking glass here.

Even at $200,000, Sam arguably had $50,000 in equity. This still would have put him $10,000 over the $40,000 exemption equity limit his state allowed. Sam's next trick was to account for selling costs as part of his home's value. When Sam filled out his petition and schedules, he allotted 8 percent for selling costs, since that would be what the trustee would have to expend if she sold Sam's house.

This is a great way to get your home under the limit. If the trustee in Sam's case actually took and sold Sam's home, she would have to hire a realtor to do so. Selling and closing costs can easily equal 8 percent. Thus, $50,000 did not really reflect the actual equity in Sam's home that the trustee could get. The actual equity was $34,000, which was under the limit. Here is how actual equity is computed:

1. Calculate 8 percent of the gross value of your house. In Sam's case, 8 percent of $200,000 is $16,000. This is what it would cost the trustee to sell Sam's house.

2. Subtract that amount from the equity in your house. $16,000 from Sam's $50,000 in equity equals $34,000 in actual equity. That is the amount that the trustee could actually expect to net from selling Sam's house. As $34,000 is less than his state's $40,000 homestead exemption ceiling, Sam would be able to keep his house.

By getting a low value and deducting selling costs, Sam was able to legally reduce the amount of equity he showed in his home from $75,000 to $34,000.

If, after all of that, your house still would be over the limit, another option would be to get a home equity loan in an amount that would reduce the equity in your house to a level under your state's exemption limit. *You would then need to use the money received to buy other, exempt, property.*

Kirsty took out a home equity loan of $10,000, which reduced the equity in her house to an amount under her state's limit. She then used this $10,000 to buy some life insurance, which she needed and which was totally exempt in her state.

This sort of maneuvering, if not done properly, can have a very negative impact on your case. Be sure to continue on and read chapter 9, "Exemption Planning."

The Important Legal Concept to Remember: If you want to keep your house, you should be able to.

9

EXEMPTION PLANNING

Proper versus improper transfers
Exemption planning

If you own either non-exempt assets or assets that are worth more than your state allows, and you file Chapter 7, the trustee has the right to take and sell that property and use the proceeds to repay your creditors. That is the rule. The critical element, then, to keeping your property is to make sure that it all falls entirely under the applicable exemptions explained in the previous chapter. That is the plan.

But the best-laid plans of mice and men often go awry. If you do not use your exemptions wisely, or, even worse, use them improperly, you will lose your property. Fearing any such possible loss, many people who own non-exempt property transfer it around prior to filing in order to protect it. Either they (ostensibly) sell it (usually to someone they know) or they convert non-exempt property into exempt property.

About a year before their bankruptcy, Kamilah and Martin settled an insurance claim and received $5,000. By the time they were ready to file bankruptcy, they still had $1,000 in the bank. Knowing that their state did not have a wild card exemption that would protect cash in the bank, Kamilah and Martin decided to convert the non-exempt asset (the money) into an exempt asset. Since their state allowed a large home equity exemption, they decided to pay down their mortgage by $1,000 before they had their case filed. The non-exempt $1,000 became exempt equity.

Transforming non-exempt assets into exempt assets before filing is called **exemption planning**. Exemption planning is understandable. In fact, it is smart. It also must be done with *extreme caution*. If an improper transfer is made before a bankruptcy, the property could be lost, and the entire bankruptcy could be thrown out.

PROPER VERSUS IMPROPER TRANSFERS. Needless to say, understanding what is legal and what is not when attempting to protect property is critical to this process. Maneuvering property around is fine; fraudulently hiding it is not. What is the difference between proper maneuvering and improper fraud? The answer is: if the debtor, *with the intent to hinder, delay or defraud creditors,* transferred, removed, mutilated or concealed his or her property within one year prior to filing the petition, then the transfer may be considered fraudulent, and the discharge denied.

The key element is the *intent of the debtor*. When Kamilah and Martin used their $1,000 to pay down their mortgage, their intent was to protect a non-exempt asset. When, a month before filing, Bill sells his Mercedes roadster to his brother for $1,000, his intent is not so pure. An intent to protect an asset is acceptable, but an intent to defraud a creditor is not. It is a fine line. Arguing about intent is the kind of thing that makes lawyers a lot of money.

Intent is also difficult to prove. Some of the things a court may look at when determining whether a transfer was proper are:

• *How soon before the bankruptcy did the transaction take place?* A transfer on the eve of bankruptcy looks much more suspicious than one eight months prior.

- *How much was received for the merchandise?* A sale that net-ted fair market value looks proper; one that does not does not.
- *Was the property transferred outside the estate?* Remember that everything you own at the time of filing constitutes your estate. A sale prior to filing, therefore, diminishes your estate and looks sneaky. On the other hand, a transmutation of non-exempt into exempt assets does not reduce the net value of the estate and therefore is less apt to be deemed questionable.
- *Who received the property?* A sale of a car to a brother looks far more fishy than one to a stranger.

This does not mean that you cannot sell any property before you file. You just cannot do so if your intent was, with an eye on bankruptcy, to defraud your creditors. You may have sold a home six months ago for less than you wanted, and if some-one contests the sale, a judge may determine that the sale was not kosher, even though you had no improper intent. It is just not black or white.

Imagine that your estate prior to filing is a pie. A likely prop-er transfer is one that slices the pie in any configuration. As long as the pie remains whole, you can pretty much slice it however you want. An improper transfer may be one that takes a piece out of the pie altogether. Notice the words "may be"; even taking a piece out of the pie can be proper if done with no intent to hide assets from a creditor.

Philip could not figure out any way to protect his fishing boat, given his state's exemption rules. Instead of losing it to the trustee, Philip simply neglected to list his boat on his schedule of assets. He did not, however, forget to list on his schedule of debts Jean, the owner of the dock to whom Philip owed three months' back rent. Jean was so infuriated at being listed in the bankruptcy that she went down to the courthouse, pulled Philip's case, and discovered the omitted boat. She then called the local office of the United States Trustee. After investigating the matter, the trustee's office decided to deny Philip a discharge.

This brings up two other tangential points of interest: One, a bankruptcy is a public document. Most people will never know about your bankruptcy unless you list them as a creditor or tell them about it. Anyone who does know about your case has a right to go to court and see the contents of your petition and schedules. Two, do not lie on your paperwork.

EXEMPTION PLANNING. The point of proper exemption planning is to (re)arrange your assets in such a way that you protect most, if not all, of your assets by maximizing your exemptions without getting into trouble. Here is how:

- *Use cash wisely.* Non-exempt money can be used to purchase exempt assets. For example, small amounts of money (a few hundred dollars) can be used to purchase exempt household goods and items, as long as the resale value of those items is less than $400 each. Larger amounts of money can be used to pay down a mortgage, thereby turning non-exempt cash into exempt equity.

- *File a homestead deed.* Some states require that debtors **homestead** their houses if they want to use the homestead exemption. A homestead deed is a document that is filed in your county recorder's office. It prevents any possible foreclosure sale by any of your creditors who may file liens against your home after the homestead deed is recorded.

- *Spend your tax refund before filing.* Tax refunds are also part of your estate. If filing around tax time, and if you do not have a wild card exemption at your disposal to protect that money, you can always spend it on food, household bills, or exempt property, prior to filing your case.

· *Try to avoid getting any large sums of money for six months.* This rule is obviously difficult to control, but nevertheless equally important to know. Any sums of money you receive within six months of filing your petition, either by gift or inheritance, as a result of a divorce settlement, or as a beneficiary of a life insurance policy, become part of your bankruptcy estate. *To the extent any such money is non-exempt, you will lose it to the trustee.* So, if getting divorced, wait six months to finalize your property settlement. If someone close to you is dying and you are to be the recipient of her will and/or life insurance, have her change the beneficiary to someone besides yourself (a spouse or child, for example).

The Important Legal Concept to Remember: You can cut your estate pie whatever way you want, but be very careful when serving a piece to someone else.

vision commercials. If you know someone who has gone through bankruptcy recently, find out how she liked her attorney, whether she was treated with courtesy and respect, whether the attorney specialized in bankruptcy, whether the lawyer returned phone calls promptly, and how much money she spent.

You may be surprised to find out how many people you know have actually filed for bankruptcy. Well over one million people a year have filed for bankruptcy protection in recent years. While there certainly used to be a stigma attached to a bankruptcy filing, because of the vast increase in filings that is far less true today. Many more people you know have filed for bankruptcy, and may be willing to talk about it and recommend a good lawyer, then you ever anticipated.

Similarly, if you have a friend who is a lawyer, ask him for a recommendation, but do not hire him. If you do decide to hire an attorney to help you through a bankruptcy, you want a bankruptcy specialist. Your friend probably is not one. And even if he were, you still would not want to hire him. Not only will you need to confess many intimate, and possibly embarrassing, financial secrets to your attorney (who, by the way, has an obligation to keep them secret), but you will have to pay your friend a lot of money in the process. There is just too much room for embarrassment and hard feelings when you hire a friend. As there are many more good lawyers around than good friends, it is far better to ask your lawyer friend's opinion about whom to hire than to hire him.

If you don't know any attorneys, and don't know anyone who knows any, then it gets a bit more difficult. Try to stay away from any referral services aside from that sponsored by your local **bar association**. Other referral services, found in the Yellow Pages, usually have but one requirement of the attorneys they recommend—money. Any lawyer who pays the fee required by the referral service will probably be recommended by that service. The local bar association is an organization of local lawyers, grouped by practice area, who often have a referral service based upon expertise, not profit.

10

LAWYERS, PARALEGALS, AND LEGAL FEES

Finding a good attorney

Meeting with your attorney

What you should expect to pay

How to bargain for the lowest possible fee

Paralegals

Once you have determined that your debts will be discharged and your assets protected, the next step is to find and hire competent counsel. Again, although a bankruptcy can be done without an attorney, that is not in your best interest.

> Marty was an intelligent man who owned his own business and decided to represent himself in his bankruptcy. One creditor, who believed that he had been defrauded by Marty, hired an attorney to contest that part of Marty's bankruptcy. The judge ruled in favor of the creditor. At the end of the hearing, the judge peered over his bench and asked Marty: "Sir, I have one question for you, do you perform surgery on yourself as well?"

FINDING A GOOD ATTORNEY. The very best place to find a good attorney is from a satisfied customer. Word-of-mouth advertising will tell far more about a lawyer than a dozen tele-

III

CHAPTER 7
BANKRUPTCY

The final option is advertising. Almost all attorneys, good and bad alike, now advertise. If a Yellow Page or television ad catches your fancy, and the lawyer practices in bankruptcy, schedule an interview and go speak with him.

MEETING WITH YOUR ATTORNEY. It is a good idea to interview a few different attorneys before deciding on one, as expertise and fees can vary greatly. It will cost you nothing, and may save you a lot of money in the long run. Most bankruptcy attorneys rarely charge when meeting with a new client for the first time. Remember this: the attorney needs you more than you need him. Competition among lawyers is fierce.

Make sure to ask the following questions at this first meeting with your potential lawyer:

· How long has he been in practice?
· Does he specialize in bankruptcy?
· Will he handle your case, or will it be given to a young **associate** or **paralegal**?
· How much should you expect to pay?
· Does he foresee any problems that may increase his fee?
· Does he have any references (former clients) with whom you can speak?

The lawyer you pick will need to get a lot of information from you regarding your financial situation. He will likely have a multipage worksheet that you will need to fill out before your second meeting. Before you are allowed to get out from $50,000 in credit card debt, the court will need to see how much you own and owe, what you make and spend. That is the purpose of the worksheet.

The second meeting is usually a relatively brief one where you go over the worksheet with your attorney and pay your fees. After this meeting, your lawyer will take all the information you have given him and draft your bankruptcy paperwork. Bankruptcy courts require that your bankruptcy petition and schedules be submitted in the proper format. Between the second and third meetings, your attorney will be preparing your information in that format for your signature.

At your final meeting with your attorney, you will review your petition and schedules, and sign everything under penalty of perjury. As there is a potential $500,000 fine and five-year prison sentence should you lie (commit **perjury**) in your paperwork, make sure it is accurate. Remember, it is you, not your attorney, who is promising (by your signature) that everything is true and correct. Make sure of that before you affix your signature to your bankruptcy papers.

WHAT YOU SHOULD EXPECT TO PAY. There are two kinds of fees to be aware of when you file for bankruptcy: legal fees and **filing fees**. Filing fees are not what the attorney charges, but what the bankruptcy court charges to file your paperwork. Although the amount of filing fees changes from time to time, you can expect to pay a couple of hundred dollars. Most bankruptcy courts will allow you to pay the fee in installments if you file your bankruptcy without the aid of an attorney.

Legal fees are the bulk of what it will cost you to file for bankruptcy. These depend upon a variety of factors. The biggest factor is the amount of time that your attorney will need to put into your case. Most bankruptcy attorneys will charge you a **flat fee** for their services; that is, a set amount of money. But the flat fee is misleading. Your attorney will determine that set price based upon the amount of time he expects to put into your case. If it will take a lot of the attorney's time, the flat fee will be higher. What constitutes more time?

· *The number of creditors you have.* A bankruptcy that only involves, say, three credit cards, is far less time-consuming for an attorney than one involving twenty different creditors.
· *Secured creditors.* If the case involves surrendering real estate, or other types of negotiations with secured creditors, your attorney will charge more.

· *Complications.* Sometimes—not often, but in some cases—**litigation** is involved. That is, a creditor files a complaint with the bankruptcy court in an effort to get its debt repaid. In such cases, an attorney will charge a *substantially higher fee.* (See chapter 13, "What Can Go Wrong?") But since it will not be known until the case is ongoing whether a complaint will be filed, this is not normally part of the initial flat fee.

What all of this means is that the more creditors you have, and the more property you own, the more your bankruptcy will cost. You should expect to pay anywhere from $500 to $1,500, sometimes more, rarely less.

HOW TO BARGAIN FOR THE LOWEST POSSIBLE FEE. Lawyers are expensive. That maxim is all the more true when you are on the verge of bankruptcy. Rather than bemoan that fact, think of your legal fees as an investment. When compared with the chance to get rid of, say, $80,000 in unsecured debts, paying an attorney $1,000 should not look so bad.

And there are ways to reduce your lawyer's fee. If you are willing to do a bit of homework, it is possible to reduce your legal costs.

Mike had about $40,000 in debts from his failed business. He called one attorney, and received a fee quote of $900. Instead of hiring that lawyer, Mike decided to call several more attorneys. He asked each what they would charge for his bankruptcy. Only three would give him a rough idea over the phone. The lowest price he received was $750. Stephen, the lawyer he liked best, quoted him a fee of $800. Mike told Stephen that he would like to hire him, but that Stephen would have to beat the $750 quote Mike received from the other attorney. Stephen agreed to a fee of $700.

You will be surprised to find that lawyers might be far more willing to dicker on a fee than you might have thought.

Many debtors wonder how they will ever pay that legal fee if they cannot even pay their debts. Here is a tip on how to do it: Once you have decided to file for bankruptcy and hire an attorney, you should *stop paying all debts that will be discharged in your bankruptcy.* There is no point in throwing good money after bad. If you are going to be getting rid of all of your credit card debt anyway, then there is simply no reason to continue to make your credit card payments once you have decided to file. Use the money that you would have paid your creditors to pay for your attorney. (While it is smart to stop paying all unsecured creditors, that is not true of your secured creditors. If you will be keeping your house or car, be sure to stay current on those payments.)

PARALEGALS. If you cannot afford an attorney, then the second best way to proceed with your bankruptcy is to hire a paralegal to draft your paperwork, and handle the rest of your case yourself. But understand, a paralegal is not an attorney. A paralegal may or may not have gone to college. Certainly, he has not gone to law school (or, if he has, he has not passed the bar exam.) A paralegal cannot give legal advice and cannot represent you in court; only an attorney can do that. A paralegal is just someone who has learned how to fill out legal paperwork.

Although what paralegals can do is quite limited, what they can do can be helpful. Your bankruptcy paperwork runs about twenty or thirty pages, and must be in the proper format to be accepted by the court. It will take you countless hours to fill out the forms if you have never done it before. A paralegal can easily draft the petition and schedules for you, and will charge no more than a few hundred dollars.

The Important Legal Concept to Remember: If you can afford to hire an attorney, it is best to do so, and contrary to popular belief, fees may be negotiable. Paralegals, when used judiciously, can be of assistance too.

11

COMMENCING THE CASE

Overview of a Chapter 7 bankruptcy
Filing the paperwork
Emergency filings
Understanding your paperwork

OVERVIEW OF A CHAPTER 7 BANKRUPTCY. The actual process of going through a Chapter 7 bankruptcy is surprisingly easy for most consumer debtors. Life before bankruptcy might be quite unpleasant, considering creditor calls, no money, stress, and worry. But once you enter the bankruptcy process, all that changes. All of a sudden, the phone stops ringing and money appears.

> Michelle's life before filing was turbulent. She was desperately trying to pay the $1,000 minimum payments on her debts every month. Her creditors were calling her at work, at home, at all hours. Everything changed once her petition and schedules were filed. The phone calls stopped almost overnight, and the $1,000 she was sending to creditors every month was now hers to keep. For the first time in a long time, she was free from stress and had a little extra money at the end of every month.

You should also find that, unlike your life today, life in bankruptcy is surprisingly non-adversarial. Throughout the process you will be treated with respect and courtesy. First of all, your creditors can no longer harass you once the case has been filed and the court issues the automatic stay. Furthermore, the attorneys, trustees, and judges that you might encounter throughout the process are all professionals whose occupation is bankruptcy. They respect the process, including—in fact, especially—the debtors who make their livelihood possible.

There are basically three steps to a Chapter 7 bankruptcy case. The first is also the most time-consuming: organizing all your affairs and getting your petition and schedules drafted and filed. Among the things you will need to organize, and eventually list in your paperwork, are:

- *A list of all assets.* This includes everything of substance you own.

- *A list of all unsecured debts.* Include to whom the debts are owed, addresses, and account numbers.

- *A list of all secured debts.* This would also include an indication of what property secures the debt and your intent with regard to the property: do you want to keep it or give it back?

- *A list of income and expenditures.* This list would comprise all sources of income and a list of average monthly expenses.

After everything is prepared and filed, the court sets a time for a hearing that you will need to attend, called the **first meeting of creditors.** That meeting usually occurs about two months after your case is filed, and is the second step in the process.

The final step occurs about two months after that hearing, when you get your discharge in the mail ending your case and officially discharging you from your legal liability to repay the debts listed in your schedules. This entire process, from filing to hearing to discharge, normally takes about four months, sometimes three, rarely six.

FILING THE PAPERWORK. A bankruptcy case is commenced when you file your petition and schedules with the court, and pay the appropriate fee. The filing fee is the same whether you are filing alone or as husband and wife. Bankruptcy courts are divided into geographical districts and are normally located in the federal courthouse of each particular district.

For many people, one of the best things about bankruptcy is the automatic stay. As discussed in chapter 5, "A Bankruptcy Primer," immediately and automatically upon the filing of your case, the court issues an *order halting all collection activities against you.*

Jose was having a very bad week. Not only was he due in small claims court on Friday to defend himself against a recent car accident he had gotten into, but his car was on the verge of being repossessed. Instead of losing his car *and* the suit, he filed bankruptcy on Wednesday. The court date was canceled and his lender stopped all repossession actions.

The stay remains in effect for the duration of your case. In very rare circumstances, a creditor can get it lifted and proceed against you (see chapter 13, "What Can Go Wrong?"), but for most people, the stay begins the healing.

EMERGENCY FILINGS. Organizing all of your information and then having it put in the proper format takes several days, at least. But sometimes you do not have several days. Sometimes, in order to get the stay, a case must be filed immediately.

An **emergency filing** is needed where your wages are about to be garnisheed, your home is about to be foreclosed upon, your car is about to be repossessed, or you are about to go to trial. In cases like these, and many others, there may not be enough time to organize everything and get it drafted and filed, before the threatened collection action is to take place.

Cognizant of the fact that some debtors need *immediate* relief, bankruptcy courts allow a debtor to commence a case by filing a "skeleton" petition and schedules. Instead of the normal twenty-odd pages which comprise most filings, a skeleton filing requires only that the debtor pay the filing fee, file the two-page petition, and at least an abbreviated list of creditors; even just listing the one creditor who is threatening the feared action will do. An attorney can draft a skeleton petition and schedule in about fifteen minutes. With the proper forms, you should be able to do it in under an hour.

If you require an emergency filing, make sure to bring at least five copies of the documents you are filing with you when you file your case (although different districts do have different requirements as to the number of copies needed). The court will give you back one copy. On your copy will be a stamp which states your case number, the time and date for your first meeting of creditors (also called a **341 hearing**) and the magical words "relief ordered" or something similar. That means that the automatic stay has been ordered and you are safe.

It is not enough to just file the skeleton, though. It often takes a week or more for your creditors to get notice of the case, so be sure to *call whoever it is that is about to take action against you and tell them that you filed for bankruptcy protection.* Give them your case number and explain that a stay has been ordered. If you are due in court, be sure to go down to the clerk before your case is to be heard and show her your bankruptcy paperwork. If your house is about to be foreclosed upon, call the agent in charge of the sale and tell her about your filing. *If no one knows about your filing, the stay is not going to be of much use.* Also, be sure to have your case number handy, as that is what will get people's attention.

It is important to know that any action taken by a creditor in violation of the stay is void. A creditor who takes action after the stay, *even if it did not know of the stay at the time the action was taken,* is required to put matters back to where they were before the action was taken. Thus, for example, a creditor that forecloses on your house in violation of the stay is required to deed the property back to you and put you back in possession, until (and if) it gets permission from the bankruptcy court to foreclose.

You are required to file the rest of your papers within fifteen days from the date of your initial filing. Although most courts and trustees are fairly flexible on this matter, if your papers are not filed, at least by the time your 341 hearing is scheduled, *the judge will* **dismiss** *your case.*

UNDERSTANDING YOUR PAPERWORK. Whether you draft your paperwork yourself or have an attorney draft it for you, it looks intimidating. Actually, it is quite easy to understand. A bankruptcy is made up of a petition, schedules which list your financial situation, a statement of financial affairs, an alphabetical listing of all creditors (called a **matrix**), and a summary of the paperwork filed.

Look at the top of any page in your bankruptcy and you will see a sort of headline in bold. That headline is then detailed in the rest of the page. For example, near the front of your paperwork will be a headline called "Schedule A—Real Property." Below will be a detailed description of all real estate you own, where it is located, what is worth, how much you owe, and so on. Each page of your bankruptcy is similarly laid out.

Your bankruptcy will consist of the following pages and information:

· *Petition.* The petition is the first two pages of your bankruptcy. It lists your name (and that of your spouse if filing jointly), any other names you may have recently used (business names, maiden names), your address, Social Security number, and other relevant information. You will sign it on page two, verifying the truthfulness of the information contained therein.

- *Schedule A—Real Property.* You already know this one: a detailed description of all real estate you own, where it is located, and so on.
- *Schedule B—Personal Property.* Here you list household goods, bank accounts, clothes, jewelry, guns, IRAs, stocks, patents, cars, **tools of the trade**, animals, everything.
- *Schedule C—Property Claimed As Exempt.* This is the property you intend to protect. Most consumer debtors should not lose property in their bankruptcy. It all it depends upon your state's exemption laws. (See chapter 7, "Protecting Your Personal Property.")
- *Schedule D—Creditors Holding Secured Claims.* Here you list all secured debts, like car and home loans.
- *Schedule E—Creditors Holding Unsecured Priority Claims.* This seemingly confusing category includes items you would probably rather not think about—taxes, government fines, alimony, that sort of thing. While not normally dischargeable, they must be listed nonetheless.
- *Schedule F—Creditors Holding Unsecured Nonpriority Claims.* These are the debts you will be getting rid of—your unsecured debts, such as credit cards, old bills, and so on. Be sure to provide accurate addresses for all creditors to ensure that they get notice of your bankruptcy.
- *Schedule G—Executory Contracts and Unexpired Leases.* This page consists of any leases that may be in effect at the time of filing, or any contracts that have yet to be fulfilled (that is what "executory" means). For example, a house painter who files a business bankruptcy would list all ongoing contracts here. Consumers would list residential and automobile contracts here.
- *Schedule H—Codebtors.* A **codebtor** is someone who is also responsible for any of the debts you list, but who is not filing with you; for example, your husband (if you are filing separately), or your grandfather who cosigned a car loan for you.

- *Schedule I—Current Income of Individual Debtors.* Here you list your job, how much money you make every month, how much is taken out of your monthly paycheck, and sources of any other income (pension, trust fund, etc.).
- *Schedule J—Current Expenditures of Individual Debtors.* Your last schedule requires that you give the court an idea of how much you spend every month on rent, utilities, food, recreation, insurance, car payments, and so on You *do not* list what you have been spending on credit cards and other sorts of debts, as those will be discharged, and in any case, by the time you file, you should not be paying them anymore.
- *Declaration Concerning Debtor's Schedules.* You sign, under penalty of perjury, that the schedules are true, complete, and accurate.

While this information must be thorough and correct, here is an important tip: budgets (schedule J) are flexible, and you want to show a budget that roughly equals your income, if at all possible and within the bounds of truth and reasonableness. If you bring home $2,000 a month, but only show a budget of $1,000 a month, then the trustee of your case may force you to **convert** your case to a Chapter 13. The trustee's theory would be that with $1,000 a month left over, you could likely pay back your creditors at least 50 percent of what you owe them, over the course of a three-year Chapter 13 plan. A Chapter 13 simply makes no sense if it can be avoided. The whole point of this is to start anew, debt free, as soon as feasible, not three years from now. *You want to avoid a Chapter 13 if at all possible.*

While each judicial district calculates the numbers very differently, the following is a useful yardstick.

1. Look at schedules I and J (income and expenses) and calculate how much you say you have left over every month. You might show nothing left over; many people still are upside down even after filing bankruptcy.

2. Multiply that number times thirty-six months.

3. If your total equals at least half of your unsecured debt, then you might end up in a Chapter 13. For example:

> Sandra had unsecured debts totaling $30,000. She made $2,500 a month, and even giving herself a generous budget, spent $2,000 a month. Her left over money, $500 a month x 36 months = $18,000. As $18,000 is more than half of $30,000, Sandra might end up in a Chapter 13.

It is important to understand that every area of the country calculates this figure very differently. In some places, for example, if you have *any* money left over in your budget, you will be forced into a Chapter 13.

The key, then, to having your case go through without a conversion, is to have your budget be as high as possible, within the bounds of truthful testimony.

There are four more documents that come after your schedules. They are:

· *Statement of financial affairs.* In this multipage document, you essentially give the court an idea of your recent financial dealings. You list your gross income for the past few years, any repossessions, foreclosures or lawsuits in the past year, losses due to fire, theft, or gambling (which are dischargeable), transfers of property in the past year, property held in safe deposit boxes, and any recent prior addresses. Businesses must also list inventories, accountants, partners, and so on. This statement too is signed under penalty of perjury.

· *Statement of intention.* It is here that you indicate what you want to do with your secured property—keep it or surrender it.

· *Matrix.* This is an alphabetical listing of all creditors that the court uses to notify them of your bankruptcy. Some courts require that the matrix also be given on computer disk. Check the requirements in your area.

· *Summary of schedules.* Finally, there is a one-page sheet that summarizes all preceding pages, especially your income, expenditures, assets, and debts, also signed under penalty of perjury.

The Important Legal Concept to Remember: The most complicated part of a Chapter 7 is organizing everything and putting it in the proper format. Once your bankruptcy is filed, your financial situation will be a lot easier.

12

HOW THE CASE PROCEEDS

The hearing
Dealing with secured creditors
Amending your papers
Lien avoidance motions
The discharge

THE HEARING. About a month or two after your case is filed, you are *required* to attend a hearing before the bankruptcy trustee who is overseeing your case, called the first meeting of creditors, or a 341 hearing. It helps to know that the first meeting of creditors is misnamed—there is rarely a second or third meeting of creditors. Also, it is a *meeting*. It is not a trial nor a hearing before a judge. It is an informal meeting, and actually quite painless.

The purpose of the meeting is twofold. First, it allows the trustee to ask you a few questions about your case. He will ask about your assets (whether you are hiding anything or have improperly transferred anything recently). He will also likely have a few questions about your schedules. You will not be unmercifully grilled or asked to explain why you are in bankruptcy. In fact, no one usually cares why or how you got here. The trustee is far more interested in whether there may be some non-exempt assets for him to seize.

Second, the meeting is a chance for any of your creditors who care to show up to ask you some questions about your assets and debts. Another reason why the first meeting of creditors is so poorly named is that creditors almost never show up. You have a constitutional right to declare bankruptcy. Unless you commit some sort of bankruptcy fraud or equally grievous offense (see chapter 13, "What Can Go Wrong?"), your case will go through and you will get your discharge. Because there is nothing creditors can do to stop it if you have acted legally, they rarely bother to show up. Your entire hearing should last about five minutes.

DEALING WITH SECURED CREDITORS. Normally, the only creditors who do bother to attend are secured creditors holding a **purchase money security interest** in some of your property. That is legalese for a creditor like Sears or J.C. Penny that holds a security interest in various items you may have recently purchased from them using their credit card. Buried deep in the credit application you signed at Sears is a paragraph ostensibly giving Sears a security interest in large items you buy there. Items such as small household goods, clothes, or shoes are not secured. Larger things like furniture or electronic equipment are secured. These creditors are at the hearing to try to get you to sign reaffirmation agreements. (Note that if you bought the item at Sears, or some other similar store, using a Visa or Mastercard, the debt is *unsecured*. Such credit cards normally do not have a security agreement as part of their application process.)

It is not always a good idea to sign such reaffirmation agreements. Recall that debtors normally have three options with regard to secured merchandise: reaffirmation, redemption, and surrender. In some states, retention is also an option. The problem with reaffirmation agreements is that they renew the personal liability of the debtor for the debt, liability that is otherwise discharged in the bankruptcy. *Debtors are not required by law to sign reaffirmation agreements.*

You may be asking yourself, am I not obliged to reaffirm that secured debt with Sears if I want to keep the property? The answer is no.

> Jerry bought a $1,000 refrigerator at Sears with his Sears card. The next year, he filed for Chapter 7. At the first meeting of creditors, the representative from Sears told him that if he did not sign a reaffirmation, Sears would take the refrigerator back because it is secured merchandise.

It is true that Sears does have a security interest in the refrigerator and does have the right, after the bankruptcy, to reclaim its property. While Sears could not sue Jerry for the cost of the refrigerator (his liability for it being discharged when his case ends), it could come and get the refrigerator after the case concludes. If Jerry wants to keep the refrigerator, Sears will tell him that the reaffirmation must be signed. Given this fact, many people choose to reaffirm their debt.

But they probably should not. What happens if Jerry neither reaffirms nor surrenders the refrigerator, and after his case is over, Sears comes to get its refrigerator back and Jerry refuses to let them in his house? Sears will then have to have its attorney go to state court and get a judicial order allowing Sears to take the property. How many thousands of dollars will that cost Sears? It simply is not cost-effective in most cases for Sears, or any secured creditor of fairly small amounts, to do so (unless it wants to make an example out of you, which sometimes happens).

Whether or not you should sign the reaffirmation depends upon what kind of risk taker you are. If you are willing to gamble that your secured creditor will not go to the effort to get its merchandise back (sometimes they do, sometimes they don't), then do not sign the reaffirmation. You may be able to keep the refrigerator without paying a penny more. And then again, you may not.

If, on the other hand, you really want to keep the merchandise, and you do not want to take the chance of losing it later, then you should probably sign the new contract. If you do so, you should *insist that the reaffirmed amount be only what the merchandise would be worth at the time of filing*, that is, its fair market value (what a willing buyer would pay a willing seller for the merchandise today). Reaffirming for the entire amount is unnecessary.

Here's why: secured claims in bankruptcy are only secured up to the fair market value of the property. Even though Jerry owes Sears $1,000, if the fair market value of that refrigerator is actually $500, then Sears's security interest is only that amount. The other $500 that Jerry owes would be unsecured, and as you know, unsecured debts are fully dischargeable. If Jerry signed a reaffirmation for $1,000, he would be taking on $500 worth of debt that would otherwise be discharged in his bankruptcy.

Many secured creditors of large items, such as cars and homes, do not ask for reaffirmation agreements, although some might. Those that do not require one simply assume that you will continue to make your scheduled monthly payments throughout the bankruptcy. If you do not, they will take back their property. When you continue to make your scheduled monthly payments throughout your bankruptcy without signing any new agreements, it is called retaining the merchandise. Unlike reaffirmation agreements, the beauty of retention is that you keep the merchandise without taking on any new financial liability. So, *try to avoid signing reaffirmations.*

A better bet, if you can afford it, is to redeem the property. Redemption requires that you pay a lump sum for the merchandise, normally the fair market value, sometimes even less. Redemption beats reaffirmation because you take on no new obligations. Pay the money, say thank you very much, and say good-bye.

Reaffirmation, redemption, and retention require that you pay for the property. If you want to rid yourself of the debt altogether, then you will need to voluntarily give the property back, which is called surrender. If you owe $10,000 for a car worth

$5,000, you might want to surrender it back to the finance company and have the debt discharged entirely. Similarly, if you do not want that refrigerator anymore and do not want to continue to pay for it, let Sears come pick it up. If the value of your house has dropped dramatically and you owe far more than it is worth, you might consider surrendering it in your bankruptcy. (Surrendering a home might have severe tax consequences, so you are strongly advised to speak with a bankruptcy professional before doing so.)

One surprising advantage of surrendering property is that it normally takes a few months to organize a time and date for the surrender. While you are waiting to give the property back, you can usually keep using it without paying for it. You can stay in your home without paying the mortgage for a few months. You can keep driving the car without making payments. Be cautioned, however, not to do this for too long. The actual rule is that a debtor is supposed to act upon his statement of intention (reaffirm, redeem, or surrender) within forty-five days of the filing, although it is a rarely enforced rule, and one without penalty.

Also, if you play this keep-the-property-and-don't-pay game too long—say, more than two months—the creditor will take action to get it back. He will go before the bankruptcy court with a motion for **relief from stay**, which is a request that the stay be lifted for this creditor as to this merchandise. (See chapter 13, "What Can Go Wrong?") You may end up with unwanted, and nondischargeable, attorneys' fees.

AMENDING YOUR PAPERS. It sometimes happens that people discover a mistake, or want to make a change, in their paperwork after their case has been filed. Maybe you realize that you forgot to list a creditor, or gave an incorrect address for one. Possibly, you failed to list an asset. Perchance, you changed your mind as to your intention with regard to a secured debt. Whatever the reason, bankruptcy procedure allows you to **amend** your schedules at any time before you receive your discharge.

Amending your papers is fairly simple. You will need to draft the amended schedule on an official bankruptcy form (like the one that was originally filed), and fill out an amendment cover sheet. Most local bankruptcy courts have one at the clerk's office. On it, you write in your name and case number and indicate the type of amendment you are filing. If you are adding a creditor, you will need to pay a little bit of money. Make five copies (usually) of the amendment and cover sheet, and file it with the court.

If you are adding a creditor, and the creditors' meeting has already been held, then you may need to schedule a second meeting of creditors, although it depends upon the rules of the district where you live. If you do, either you or the court (again, depending upon your locale) will send a notice to all creditors of the new meeting time and date. Check with your court to find out the exact procedure.

You will also need to file a change of address form with the court if you move while you are in bankruptcy. Throughout your case, the court mails important information to you: a notice of filing (including the automatic stay order), a notice of no distribution (if your assets are completely exempt), and most importantly, your discharge order. The discharge order is something that you will want to keep safe for some time; it prevents any of your creditors whose debt was discharged from coming after you once the case is over. So you want the court to be able to find you if you move.

LIEN AVOIDANCE MOTIONS. There are many financial benefits to filing bankruptcy—the automatic stay, the chance to get out of bad contracts, and having your debts discharged being but three of them.

Another, equally powerful, albeit somewhat more limited, tool, is called a **lien avoidance motion**. A lien avoidance motion does exactly what its name implies: it gets rid of liens on your house.

Prior to filing bankruptcy, LaVonne was sued in small claims court and lost, and afterward, the creditor recorded a judicial lien against LaVonne's home. As with all liens, if LaVonne ever sold her house, the lien would get paid before LaVonne saw any proceeds from the sale. LaVonne would have been stuck with this debt after her bankruptcy, except for the fact that she filed a lien avoidance motion with the bankruptcy. The judge ruled in her favor, the lien was released, and LaVonne's liability for this debt was discharged.

Not all liens can be avoided. A mortgage cannot be avoided, for example, nor can tax liens, or secured auto payments. Only the following liens can be avoided.

- *Judgment liens.* As in the case of LaVonne, a judgment lien is created when someone sues you, wins, and files a lien against your property.
- *Nonpossessory, nonpurchase-money security interests.* Translated, this is a lien created by a lender who loans money in exchange for a security interest in household goods and items you own.

Well before his bankruptcy, Stan was in dire need of some extra cash. He called around and found a company called Easy Money Financial that was willing to lend him $2,500 if Stan would grant Easy Money a security interest in his furniture, stereo, and television. Stan agreed, and a nonpossessory, nonpurchase-money security interest was created in favor of Easy Money. If Stan wants to discharge this debt in his bankruptcy, he will need to file a lien avoidance motion.

The idea behind lien avoidance is that the bankruptcy code wants to give debtors a fresh start, and that is made more difficult when otherwise exempt property is impaired by a lien.

Unlike getting rid of the rest of your debts in a Chapter 7, avoiding a lien is not automatic. The debtor (or her counsel) must bring the motion before the court, and the judge must order the lien released. Each jurisdiction around the country has different rules with regard to what is required to avoid a lien. For example, some districts require that the motion be brought fairly quickly after filing, such as before the creditors' meeting.

While an attorney's help is advisable, if you must file the lien avoidance motion yourself, go down to your local bankruptcy court, find a similar motion, and copy it, changing the facts where appropriate.

THE DISCHARGE. The meeting of creditors is over very quickly. A negotiation with your secured creditors may take place in the hall or outside the courthouse for about five minutes. You get to go home.

In most cases, absolutely nothing happens in the case for about two months, save for maybe a lien avoidance motion. Then, about sixty days after the meeting, your discharge appears in the mail. That is it. Your case is over, your debts have been discharged, and you get your fresh start.

The Important Legal Concept to Remember: From start to finish, a Chapter 7 bankruptcy case should last only about four months. Once the bankruptcy is filed, debtors usually have little else to do but attend the ill-named first meeting of creditors and deal with any secured creditors. The discharge is surprisingly quick and easy to get.

13

WHAT CAN GO WRONG?

Problems with the automatic stay
Credit card fraud
Preferential payments
Having your case converted
Having your case dismissed
Having your discharge denied

Most consumer Chapter 7 bankruptcies proceed without a hitch. As long as you are honest in your petition and schedules, your discharge will come in the mail about two months after the meeting of creditors. For most debtors, this process from filing to hearing to discharge is seamless and surprisingly simple.

In a small number of cases, a wrinkle or two may arise, but presents no serious threat to the discharge. In very, very few cases, serious problems erupt, threatening the entire process.

PROBLEMS WITH THE AUTOMATIC STAY. The stay remains in effect for the duration of your case; you know that already. Yet sometimes a creditor wants to continue collection activities despite the stay. Usually, a creditor will *request permission* from the court to continue collection proceedings. That is legal. Sometimes, however, the creditor continues to proceed against the debtor, but does so *without* court permission. That is not. There are times when the creditor can request relief from stay so that it can continue its collection activities. If the court agrees, the stay is lifted *as to this creditor only*, and the threatened action becomes reality.

Shamshad was two months behind on her mortgage and on the verge of foreclosure when she filed Chapter 7. She intended to catch up on her mortgage with the extra money she anticipated having after filing, but she did not. A month after filing, she was three months behind on her mortgage. Her mortgage company went to court requesting relief from stay. Since she was continuing to fall behind on her mortgage, the court granted the motion, and the automatic stay was lifted as to this creditor. The mortgage company then foreclosed on Shamshad's house.

A relief from stay motion cannot be sought just because a creditor is angry at being included in a bankruptcy. If that were true, then every creditor would file a similar motion. There are only a few, specific circumstances where a relief from stay will be sought and granted:

1. *Lack of adequate protection.* Normally, if you have no equity in a secured item, like a car or house, and you stop making payments, the court will grant relief from stay because the lender's interest in the property is not being protected.

2. *For cause.* The stay stops *all* proceedings against you. If you are involved in a dispute unrelated to your bankruptcy— child custody, for example, the stay can be lifted as to that matter.

If a creditor brings a relief from stay motion against you, he is required to give you notice of the date and time for the hearing, and you have a right to defend yourself and oppose the stay.

The other way the stay may be in play occurs where a creditor simply *ignores* it, does not request relief from stay, and continues to harass the debtor as if nothing has happened. The collection agency does not stop calling, a creditor files suit, that sort of thing. Such actions constitute **contempt of court**. The automatic stay is a federal court order, and bankruptcy judges do not take kindly to being ignored.

If one of your creditors is violating the stay, you have two options. First, you could simply call the creditor and explain that he is violating a federal court order, which he may not know, and he may just stop. This is certainly easier and cheaper than the second option—having your attorney file a contempt of court motion against the creditor.

For a contempt of court motion to succeed, the debtor must be able to prove

1. that the creditor knew of the stay, and
2. that the creditor intentionally violated the stay, and
3. that the violation was serious.

A creditor, knowing of a bankruptcy, who continues to send the debtor a monthly bill will not get in trouble because that is not a significant violation. An auto repossession, however, would be considered contempt of court.

Contempt of court is a serious matter. A creditor who loses a violation of stay motion will likely end up paying the debtor for any expenses his actions caused, attorney fees, and possibly punitive damages. Punitive damages are designed to punish the perpetrator and teach him a lesson. They can run anywhere from $100 to $10,000 or more, depending upon the circumstances.

CREDIT CARD FRAUD. While a creditor cannot sue you while you are in bankruptcy *outside* of bankruptcy court (because of the stay), he can, *inside* of bankruptcy court. But, as with relief from stay motions, the creditor must have a good reason to sue you. In almost all cases where this occurs, the creditor files suit alleging that the debtor committed **credit card fraud** and therefore should be denied a discharge as to *this particular debt*.

About a month before she filed for bankruptcy, Tamar's transmission died. She took a $2,000 cash advance off her Armata Visa and fixed the car. That debt broke the camel's back, and Tamar filed Chapter 7. After the meeting of creditors, Armata filed suit against Tamar, alleging credit card fraud. Although she never intended to defraud anyone, it would have been too costly for Tamar to fight the suit. She got her discharge for all debts except the Armata card, and agreed to pay them back $1,500 at $100 a month.

Here is the important rule: If, in the sixty days before filing, you charged more than $1,000 on a luxury good or item, or received a cash advance for more than $1,000, *on any one card*, the law **presumes** that you committed credit card fraud. Debts created by fraud are nondischargeable if the creditor objects, and wins.

It helps to think of a presumption this way: When you are arrested, you are presumed innocent until proven guilty. Here, with a large charge right before filing, you are presumed guilty until proven innocent. Because this is one of the few areas of bankruptcy law that especially favors creditors, expect a so-called **nondischargeability complaint** to be filed against you if applicable to your situation.

If a nondischargeability complaint is filed against you, it is not the end of the world, but it will cost you money. Fighting the allegations will require an expensive lawyer. Settling will leave you with a nondischargeable debt. Either way, you will likely have to pay someone.

Here's a good tip if you are worried about a nondischargeability complaint possibly being filed against you: If you have not filed your case yet, and you have recently charged more than $1,000 on a single credit card, *wait for sixty days after the large charge before filing your case*. This gets you out of the "presumption period" and makes a lawsuit less likely. Understand that this does not mean that a creditor still cannot sue you; if one thinks you committed some sort of fraud, it can. A lawsuit can be filed against you even if the charge is outside of the presumption period. It is just *far less likely* to occur after the sixty-day period has elapsed.

> Jessica knew she would have to file bankruptcy within the next year or so. She therefore decided to take a risk and took a $5,000 cash advance from one of her unsecured credit cards. She used the money to pay off her secured car loan. When she filed bankruptcy eight months later, she knew that a nondischargeability complaint might be filed by that credit card company and she would have to pay the $5,000 back. The complaint was never filed, the debt was discharged, and Jessica owned the car free and clear when the case was over.

The large charge can occur at any time before the debtor files to be deemed questionable. But, once outside the sixty-day presumption period, the law neither favors nor disfavors the creditor, so complaints regarding charges in that time frame are less likely to succeed.

When a court or a creditor examines a charge, or series of charges, to determine whether or not it was fraudulent, one of the main things looked at is the intent of the debtor to repay the debt. If the debtor has shown no intent to repay the debt, then a complaint is far more likely because the transaction looks more fraudulent. But if the debtor has been keeping current on his payments, then proving that he actually intended to defraud someone is far more difficult. Accordingly, *if you have a questionable transaction, be sure to keep paying the bill until you file.*

One final tip: Many times a creditor will write either to your attorney or to you, if you are acting in pro per, stating that it has solid grounds to file a nondischargeability complaint against you. The letter will request that you sign an attached reaffirmation agreement and avoid the hassle and expense of a nondischargeability suit. Do not be fooled. It costs almost nothing to have an attorney draft such a letter and reaffirmation. If the creditor actually has the goods on you, it will file the complaint before your case is concluded. If it does not, it won't. Call their bluff. If a complaint is filed, *then* you can negotiate with them. Doing so beforehand is unnecessary and unwise.

PREFERENTIAL PAYMENTS. Another issue that may arise before your discharge is that of preferential payments. Bankruptcy law wants you to treat all of your creditors equally. It does not want to see you favoring one creditor over another, maybe paying back your brother before you file, but not Mastercard.

When you have paid, or transferred, money worth more than $600 to any single creditor in the *ninety days* before filing, the law considers it a preferential payment. Similarly, if you have paid $600 or more to any friend or relative in the *year* before you filed, this too is considered a preferential payment. You are preferring one creditor over another.

When a preferential payment has been made, the trustee has the right to go to the party who received the payment and get the money back. The money is then sent to your creditors proportionally. While you may not care when your trustee attempts to get that $1,000 back from Armata Visa, you may if he attempts to get it back from your mom.

Understand that there is nothing fraudulent about paying off a favorite creditor; you will still get your discharge. You just may find, though, that someone close to you is not too happy when the trustee comes after that money.

HAVING YOUR CASE CONVERTED. One of the questions that your trustee will likely ask you at your hearing is whether anything has changed since the filing of your bankruptcy. Maybe you got a new job or lost a job, maybe you received some unanticipated money or lost some money. Your trustee is especially curious to find out if you are making any more money at the time of your hearing than at the time of your filing. If the trustee determines that you are making enough money to pay your creditors back, then one unfortunate problem that you may encounter is that your case might get converted into a Chapter 13 against your wishes.

One of the trustee's jobs is to maximize any possible return to your creditors. If you are in the typical **no-asset case** (meaning everything you own is exempt), then there is nothing to return to your creditors. But by converting your case into a Chapter 13, the trustee can get some money for your creditors, since you will be forced to pay them back for at least three years.

If this does happen to you, and you do not wish to be in a Chapter 13, your first recourse would be to move to have your case dismissed, in which case you would receive no discharge, and your creditors could again start to take actions to collect their money. Or, you could simply make no payments to the Chapter 13 trustee after your case is converted, and that trustee will dismiss your case for you.

While a possibility, conversion occurs in only a rare number of cases, usually where the debtor's income far outstrips his expenditures. This only serves to highlight that when you initially fill out your budget (schedule I), be sure to make it as high as reasonably possible to avoid this possibility.

HAVING YOUR CASE DISMISSED. There is also the remote chance that your case may be dismissed. This occurs only where your filing fees have never been paid, if you fail to file all appropriate papers (as in the case of an emergency skeleton filing in which the remainder of the schedules were never filed), if you fail to attend the first meeting of creditors (attending that hearing is mandatory), or if you filed your case in bad faith.

If your case is dismissed, it will likely be dismissed "with prejudice," meaning you cannot file again for 180 days.

HAVING YOUR DISCHARGE DENIED. The second worst possible thing that could happen to your case is to have your discharge denied. (The worst is criminal sanctions for committing perjury.) The entire point of bankruptcy is to get the discharge, relieving you from any further personal liability for the scheduled debts. In almost every case, the discharge is automatic, arriving about four months after commencement of the case. In a very rare number of cases, the discharge may be denied. Note that here, unlike with the aforementioned credit card nondischargeability complaint, the *entire discharge* is at stake, not just the discharge as it relates to one individual debt.

Denial of discharge results from either the trustee or a creditor's filing a complaint with the bankruptcy court. If proved with "clear and convincing" evidence (an exceptionally tough standard to meet), discharge can be denied for any of the following:

1. *Intentional concealment, transfer or destruction of property.* The most common reason, this occurs where a debtor knowingly hides or sells non-exempt assets.

2. *Dishonesty in connection with the bankruptcy case.* Debtors who commit perjury (either in their paperwork or at their hearing), who present false claims, who fail to adequately explain the loss of estate assets, who conceal or destroy important financial documents, or who withhold records can be denied a discharge.

3. *Receipt of a discharge in the preceding six years.* You can only file bankruptcy every six years. If you received a discharge within the last six years, this one will be denied.

Denial of a discharge is a radical judicial remedy that is used in only the most egregious of cases. Be honest and all should go well.

The Important Legal Concept to Remember: Almost all cases conclude without any significant problems. It is when you lie during this process that you can expect difficulty.

CHAPTER 13 BANKRUPTCY

14

CHAPTER 13 MADE EASY

The purpose of a Chapter 13
Getting caught up with secured creditors
Protecting non-exempt assets
Other reasons
Reasons not to choose a Chapter 13
Advantages and disadvantages

THE PURPOSE OF A CHAPTER 13. If a Chapter 7 is the Hollywood blockbuster of bankruptcies intended for the masses, then a Chapter 13 is more akin to a small foreign film. It is not for everyone and not seen by that many people, but it has its place and is important for those who do see it.

Certainly, most people are better off filing a Chapter 7. Yet for some people, a Chapter 7 either will not get rid of their debts or will cause them to lose non-exempt property. Chapter 13s are also far more common in some parts of the country than in others. In some places, judges and districts try to guide their debtors into Chapter 13s by implementing various local rules intended to make Chapter 13s more common (which is perfectly legal). For example, if you show any significant room in your budget (schedule J), then you may be forced into a Chapter 13.

A Chapter 13 is similar to a Chapter 7 in that the general process is roughly similar in both types of cases. The stay halts all actions against the debtor. The schedules list all assets and debts. The discharge wipes out the debtor's personal liability for those debts. The difference relates mostly to the length of the case and how secured debts are handled.

Instead of wiping out all dischargeable debts in a few short months as a Chapter 7 does, a Chapter 13 lasts for *at least* three years, and possibly up to five years, depending upon the circumstances. During that time, the debtor promises to pay a certain amount of money *every month* through a Chapter 13 plan to the Chapter 13 trustee, who in turn uses the money to pay back the debtor's creditors.

Since most people do not want to be in bankruptcy for four months, let alone four years, you had better be awfully sure that it makes sense for you before plunging in. And whereas a Chapter 7 can be handled without an attorney if need be, a Chapter 13 almost always requires the assistance of counsel. Debtors should be especially wary of *non-lawyers* who counsel that a Chapter 13 can be done without the assistance of an attorney.

GETTING CAUGHT UP WITH SECURED CREDITORS. Most people file a Chapter 13 because they are behind on a secured debt like a car loan, but far more often, a home loan, and they see no way of getting caught up during a Chapter 7. This is the most common, and usually the best, reason, why a person would choose to file a Chapter 13 bankruptcy over a Chapter 7. *A Chapter 13 is the only way to catch up mortgage or auto arrears in a bankruptcy; a Chapter 7 will not wipe out those debts.*

Everything was fine for Spencer and Aviva until Aviva lost her job. They fell $5,000 and three months behind on their mortgage, and their house was on the verge of foreclosure, when they met with an attorney who recommended a Chapter 13 bankruptcy. They had the case filed the next day. The sale was called off. Spencer and Aviva then spent the next three years paying the Chapter 13 trustee roughly $150 a month to catch up on their past-due mortgage, while simultaneously staying current with their ongoing mortgage payments.

You can certainly bet that if Spencer and Aviva had tried to get their lender to accept a three-year repayment schedule *outside of bankruptcy*, they would have had no luck whatsoever. But by filing Chapter 13, they were able to legally force their lender to accept the repayment plan, whether it wanted to or not. As long as they make all scheduled payments to the trustee, they will get to keep their home. Because a Chapter 13 creates a repayment schedule (which is what the plan actually is), a Chapter 13 is also called a reorganization.

If you want to reorganize your mortgage arrears and keep your home by filing a Chapter 13, you better be sure that you *really* want to keep your house, and that your house is *really* worth keeping.

Josefina owned her home for only two years before she fell behind on the payments. Although she wanted to keep it, she had bought the house at the height of the market and therefore had no equity in it. Since her prospects for recouping her investment looked slim, she decided to let the foreclosure go through rather than repay the trustee for three years.

Paying a Chapter 13 trustee a set amount for a minimum of three years is no easy task. Not only will this payment to the trustee need to be made every month, but you will need to stay current with your normal monthly mortgage payments and all other regular bills as well. If you fall behind on your payments to the trustee at any point during the course of your plan, your case will be dismissed and your lender will foreclose. It is very important to realize that *roughly 50 percent of all Chap-*

ter 13 cases and plans are never finished, because making the payments seems easier (upon filing) than it actually is (say two years into the plan).

When a Chapter 13 plan becomes impossible to continue paying, debtors normally convert their case into a Chapter 7. In that case, the unsecured debts are discharged, and the house is foreclosed upon because the arrears are not fully caught up.

This is just a cautionary note to warn you that Chapter 13 is not easy for most debtors. Your house had better be worth keeping before you undertake this arduous task.

PROTECTING NON-EXEMPT ASSETS. Another common reason why a person may choose a Chapter 13 over a Chapter 7 is that a Chapter 13 allows the debtor to keep all of his assets, not just exempt assets.

> Colin owned a small antiques store. Although he certainly had enough debts to warrant a Chapter 7, he had $50,000 in collectibles that he just could not exempt, no matter how hard he tried. Had he filed a 7, his antiques would have been sold by the trustee and he would have had to go out of business. After much consideration, he decided to file a Chapter 13. He kept all of his assets and paid back his creditors over a five-year plan.

Is there a catch? But of course. One of the many requirements of a Chapter 13 is that your creditors *receive at least what they would have received had you filed a Chapter 7*. In the case of Colin, his creditors would have received at least $50,000, since that is the amount of his non-exempt assets. Accordingly, if Colin wants to keep all of his property, he must present a Chapter 13 plan that proposes to pay back at least that much. He would have to offer a plan that would pay his creditors at least $834 a month for five years ($834 x 60 months = $50,040). Of course this is a cumbersome requirement, but it is also the only way Colin could be assured of keeping his non-exempt assets. If Colin wanted to complete his bankruptcy in three years (it is his choice if he can afford it), he would need to pay $1,389 a month for thirty-six months ($1,389 x 36 = $50,004).

One other important concept of note: Although Colin would have to pay back at least $50,000, that does not necessarily mean that his creditors will get one hundred cents on the dollar. It depends upon how much secured and unsecured debt Colin has. Assuming he has only unsecured debt, if Colin owes his creditors $100,000, then, because all he is required to pay back is $50,000, each of his creditors would get 50 percent of what Colin owes them. If he owes $200,000, then all they would get back would be 25 percent. At the end of his plan, the remainder of whatever Colin owed would be discharged, just as it would have been in a Chapter 7.

Finally, the amount Colin (or any debtor) would have to pay back varies from district to district. The aforementioned test—creditors receiving at least what they would have received in a Chapter 7—is the *minimum* that a Chapter 13 debtor has to pay back to unsecured creditors. Some judicial districts require nothing more than that. Others mandate that unsecured creditors receive 100 percent of what they are owed. If Colin owes his unsecured creditors $100,000 and he lives in this sort of district, he would have to pay the trustee $1,667 a month. ($1,667 x 60 months = $100,020). Chapter 13 cases are not easy.

OTHER REASONS. There are several other reasons why someone may want to file a Chapter 13, although catching up on arrears and protecting non-exempt assets are by far the most common.

One of the most compelling reasons to file a Chapter 13 is how secured debts are handled. As in a Chapter 7, secured property can be surrendered or not. The Chapter 13 advantage is that the secured property you choose to keep need only be paid back at the fair market value of the property, *not the entire amount owed.*

Suzzane's car was worth $5,000, but she owed $10,000 on it. In her Chapter 13 plan, she proposed to pay her car lender a total of $6,500 over three years, which was the fair market value of the car, plus 10 percent interest. The other $3,500 she owed would be discharged when the Chapter 13 plan payments were completed.

A Chapter 13 is great for people who have a bad car contract but want to keep the car.

Any one of the following is also a legitimate reason for filing a Chapter 13:

· *Having received a discharge in a bankruptcy within the past six years.* If you received a Chapter 7 discharge, you must wait at least six years before filing Chapter 7 again. If you received a Chapter 13 discharge, you must wait at least six years before filing a Chapter 7 (unless you repaid your creditors at least 70 percent of what you owed them). But in either case, you can file a Chapter 13 at any time.

· *Owing back child support, alimony, student loans, etc.* If such problems are causing your wages to be garnished or otherwise making your life difficult, a Chapter 13 would allow you to repay these debts over the course of your plan. These debts, just as with home or car arrears, must be repaid fully over the course of the plan to get a discharge.

· *Being behind on taxes.* Sometimes Uncle Sam is willing to work with you regarding your tax problems, sometimes not. If your taxes are nondischargeable, as many are (see chapter 6, "Do You Have the Right Type of Debts?"), then you can always propose to repay them through a Chapter 13 plan. Since you draft the plan, this puts you back in control of the situation.

· *Wiping out debts that cannot be discharged in a Chapter 7.* One of the truly great things about a Chapter 13 is that you can get debts discharged that cannot be discharged in a Chapter

7. Debts incurred by fraud, larceny, embezzlement, credit card fraud, assault, battery, false imprisonment, or defamation are not dischargeable in a 7. But in a 13, they are treated just like any other unsecured debt, repaid normally pennies on the dollar, and discharged upon the completion of all plan payments.

REASONS NOT TO CHOOSE A CHAPTER 13. Wanting to file a Chapter 13 because you feel a moral obligation to repay your debts, while admirable, is nevertheless not smart. You are best off paying the debts outside of bankruptcy; there is no point in harming your credit any more than you have to.

If you are contemplating filing a 13 instead of a 7 because you think it might look "better" to future creditors, you are mistaken. A bankruptcy is a bankruptcy is a bankruptcy. It matters little to anyone but you what chapter you choose to file under.

Finally, if you are filing a 13 because you are afraid that losing your home in a Chapter 7 means you will never get a home loan again, you are wrong. Yes, it is true that a bankruptcy will stay on your credit report for ten years (although the common practice is for credit reporting agencies to list Chapter 13 cases for only seven years). But that is only half the story.

It is not unusual, in fact it is almost commonplace, for people who have gone through a Chapter 7 bankruptcy to get a home loan in less than *two years after they get their discharge*. The fact is, a bankruptcy is not an anathema to most mortgage lenders any longer. Not only do they know that the debtor cannot file again for at least six years, not only has the increase in filing made bankruptcies far more common on credit reports, but, surprisingly, bankruptcy makes some people *more attractive* applicants than they would have been had they not filed. Since home loans are based, at least in part, upon one's debt-to-income ratio, and since Chapter 7 bankruptcy wipes out most debts, a debtor's ratios look better, and his chances of getting the loan are improved, if he has recently received a discharge.

ADVANTAGES AND DISADVANTAGES. The advantages of filing Chapter 13 should be fairly self-evident. You are able to keep your property, make up any arrears you may have on your own terms, rid yourself of debts that you otherwise could not in a Chapter 7, and discharge your other debts. Secured car loans can be drastically rearranged in your favor. Depending upon the circumstances and the laws in your district, you may be able to get rid of unsecured debts for pennies on the dollar.

On the downside, paying the trustee back each month, every month, will surely get tiresome. Attorney fees are significantly higher in a Chapter 13 case as a lot of work has to go into the plan and the various hearings. And, as with a Chapter 7, there is no doubt your credit rating will be negatively affected. Yet, on the whole, a Chapter 13, if it applies to your situation, may be the best thing you can do for yourself.

The Important Legal Concept to Remember: A Chapter 13 can put a debtor back in control of his financial situation. But remember: at least half of all Chapter 13 debtors find it too difficult to finish paying their plan.

15

THE CHAPTER 13 PROCESS

Chapter 13 requirements
How things proceed

CHAPTER 13 REQUIREMENTS. Unlike a Chapter 7, which permits anyone to file, regardless of employment status or debt levels, a debtor contemplating a Chapter 13 must meet certain requirements. Unless you meet these prerequisites, your case will be dismissed.

1. *Be an individual with regular income.* Only individuals can file a Chapter 13. The only business entity that can file a Chapter 13 is a sole proprietorship, and even then, it can only do so in the name of the individual who owns the business. Corporations and partnerships cannot file a 13.

   And not even all individuals can file a 13. The rule is that the individual must have "regular income." This means that the individual who files must have a source of regular and stable income, usually a job, so that the court can be assured that the Chapter 13 plan payments will be made. Social Security, welfare, or owning a small business would constitute stable income, as would alimony and child support, or rental income. As unemployment benefits are for a limited duration, they probably would not constitute stable income.

2. *Have disposable income.* The heart of a Chapter 13 is the repayment plan. It follows then, that you must be able to afford plan payments. When you fill out your budget (schedules I and J), you must show that you have enough money left over at the end of every month to fund your plan. *This is very different than what you want to do in a Chapter 7.*

Monica decided to file her Chapter 13 in pro per, and did not hire an attorney. Her schedules showed an income of $1,000 a month, and expenditures of $1,000 a month. At her hearing, the trustee asked her how she planned to make the scheduled $250-a-month plan payments if she had no disposable income. Monica had no answer. Her case was dismissed shortly thereafter.

3. *Be under the debt ceiling.* In a Chapter 7, there is no limit as to how much debt you can have. You can have $5,000 in unsecured debt or $200,000. You can have $10,000 in secured debts or $1 million. It makes no difference. That is not true in a Chapter 13. In a Chapter 13, your unsecured debts cannot exceed $250,000, and your secured debts cannot exceed $750,000.

HOW THINGS PROCEED. Once you have determined that you fall within the Chapter 13 parameters and that it will solve your financial problems, things proceed in a somewhat similar fashion as in a Chapter 7.

First of all, you will need to have your Chapter 13 petition and schedules drafted and filed. In addition, you will need to file your plan, which details how much money you have left over every month and therefore how much you have to pay into the plan every month; how much total will be paid over the entire course of the plan; the percentage return you propose to pay your unsecured creditors; and how long the plan is expected to last. (See chapter 16, "How Much Will You Have to Repay?")

Jerrold owed $5,000 in mortgage arrears, and had $8,000 in credit card debt. His schedules showed income of $1,500 a month, and expenditures of $1,250 a month. His Chapter 13 plan proposed to pay all of his disposable income into the plan, $250 a month, for thirty-six months, totaling $9,000. $5,000 would be used to pay his mortgage arrears, and the other $4,000 would go to Jerrold's unsecured creditors (paying them back fifty cents on the dollar).

You will need to make your first payment into the plan within a month of filing your documents. Failure to make plan payments is the surest way of getting your case dismissed.

A month or two after everything has been filed, you will attend the first meeting of creditors, although here the name is not so inappropriate. Chapter 13 creditors' meetings often require more than one appearance. Unlike a Chapter 7 creditors' meeting, which is intended to quickly discover if there are any unlisted assets or changes in the paperwork, a Chapter 13 hearing is a chance for the trustee to go over the plan in detail. Does it meet all legal requirements? Is it proposed in good faith? Will it pay everyone back in the requisite number of months? The trustee may request that the debtor make certain changes in the plan, or may ask that certain documentation be provided.

After the meeting of creditors has been concluded, you may be required to attend two more hearings. The first is a **confirmation** hearing, where the court approves or disapproves of your plan. In some jurisdictions, this is accomplished without an actual hearing.

The second is a valuation hearing, which occurs only if a creditor objects to the value you list in your schedules for its secured merchandise. This occurs most often with an auto that has been included in the plan. A judge will decide whether your lower, or the creditor's higher, valuation of the merchandise is correct.

Sarah listed her car's value at $8,000 in her schedules, and her plan proposed to pay back only that amount, plus interest. Her lender challenged Sarah's valuation, contending that the car was worth $12,000. At the valuation hearing, the judge sided with the lender, and ordered Sarah to amend her plan so as to pay back a principal amount of $12,000, plus interest.

After the plan has been **confirmed**, payments will be due every month, and payments are made to the trustee's office. Other than that, you will probably have little substantial interaction with the trustee for the duration of your case. Once all of your plan payments have been made, you will get your discharge.

The Important Legal Concept to Remember: For most debtors, the main difference between a Chapter 13 and a Chapter 7 is that the 13 takes a lot longer and they will have to repay at least some of their debts.

16

HOW MUCH WILL YOU HAVE TO REPAY?

Best interest of the creditors test
Best effort
Calculating the plan
Failure to complete the plan

Undoubtedly, the most important question you will face in your Chapter 13 case is how much you will have to pay into the plan to get any arrears current, and all other debts discharged. It is, unfortunately, a fairly complicated, albeit necessary, analysis.

> Stuart was three months behind in his mortgage; his arrears totaled $5,000. He also had $20,000 in unsecured debt. He owned a car which was $10,000 over the exemption limit. He brought home $2,500 a month and spent $2,100 a month. Rather than lose his house, Stuart filed for Chapter 13 protection.

BEST INTEREST OF THE CREDITORS TEST. Your unsecured creditors must receive in your Chapter 13 at least what they would have received in a Chapter 7. That is called the "best interest of the creditors" test.

In Stuart's case, had he filed a Chapter 7, he would have lost his non-exempt car to the Chapter 7 trustee. So, in his Chapter 13, Stuart will have to propose a plan that will pay his unsecured creditors back at least $10,000, as that is the amount they would have received had Stuart filed a Chapter 7.

Since the main reason Stuart wants to file a Chapter 13 is to pay back his mortgage arrears, his plan will also need to include that $5,000 arrearage repayment. So, at least initially, Stuart will have to pay at least $15,000 into his plan ($10,000 for unsecured creditors and $5,000 for his secured mortgage.)

Priority debts—that is, debts owed for taxes, child support, and the like—must be part of any plan and must be repaid in full to be discharged.

BEST EFFORT. The plan has to be the very best effort that the debtor can put forth. That means that the debtor will live frugally, without expending money for luxuries. Beyond that, "best effort" varies from district to district. In some places it means that all the creditors, secured and unsecured alike, must be paid in full. In others, it means that the debtor will pledge all disposable income into the plan.

In Stuart's case, it looks like his best effort is $400 a month, since he brings home $2,500 a month and spends $2,100 a month. If he lived in a district that requires 100 percent repayment of all creditors, his plan would not be confirmed. Here is why: $400 a month, even for the maximum of sixty months, would equal only $24,000. His total debt, secured and unsecured combined, is $25,000. Since he could not pay off his debts in time and in full, even given his best effort, his plan would not get confirmed and his case would be dismissed.

Stuart fortunately lived in a district that permitted less than 100 percent repayment of unsecured creditors, as long as it was his best effort. He proposed a plan of $388 a month for thirty-six months. This would pay a total of $13,968 into the plan. His secured mortgage holder would receive 100 percent of what it is owed. His unsecured creditors, to whom he owed $20,000, would receive a total of $8,968, translating into about forty-five cents on the dollar.

At his hearing, the trustee inquired about Stuart's $400-a-month car payment. Stuart explained that he drove a new BMW. The trustee told him to sell it and buy a car with payments of no more than $300 per month. Thus, Stuart suddenly had another $100 to add into his plan—$488 a month.

In most places, as long as you propose a budget that is fair and modest (but not necessarily spartan), that pledges all available extra capital to the plan, that pays back secured and priority creditors 100 percent, and that attempts to give your unsecured creditors something, the plan will be confirmed.

CALCULATING THE PLAN.

The trustee also noted that Stuart had failed to calculate any interest for his mortgage holder, as most jurisdictions require. Stuart also forgot to add in any money for the trustee, 10 percent being the norm.

Interest and trustee fees cannot be overlooked. Instead of paying $388 a month for thirty-six months, all of a sudden, Stuart's plan looked like this:

Mortgage arrears:	$5,000
Interest on mortgage arrears:	$1,500 (10 percent a year for three years)
Amount necessary for unsecured creditors:	$10,000
Subtotal:	$16,500
Trustee fee at 10 percent:	$1,650
Total needed to be paid into plan:	$18,150

Stuart therefore proposed an amended plan in which he would pay $488 a month for thirty-seven months, totaling $18,056. His secured debt would be paid off in full, with interest, and his unsecured creditors would receive fifty cents on the dollar. The trustee would get her fee. Stuart proposed to pay the extra $94 needed to complete the plan in the 37th month ($18,056 + $94 = $18,150).

FAILURE TO COMPLETE THE PLAN. Again, no more than half of all Chapter 13 debtors ever complete their plan payments, although all assuredly enter the process with every intention of doing so. In most cases, plan payments cease because the debtor or his spouse lost a job, the debtors get divorced, or some other situation renders further plan payments impossible. When that happens, debtors can do one of the following.

1. *Modify the plan.* It is always possible to modify the plan payments as circumstances dictate. As long as everyone will still get the amount required by law (e.g., unsecured creditors receiving what they would have received in a Chapter 7, and so on), the modification should be acceptable to the trustee and creditors.

2. *Request a hardship discharge.* If a modification is not feasible, then you can apply for a special "hardship discharge." This is possible when circumstances beyond your control significantly change your financial condition, such as the death of a mate or the permanent loss of a job. If so, the bankruptcy code provides for the possibility of a discharge, *even if all plan payments have not been paid.* The only hitch is that your unsecured creditors must receive, by the time of the hardship discharge, what they would have received in a Chapter 7.

3. *Convert your case to a Chapter 7.* Debtors have an absolute right to convert their case at any time. Although you may lose your house, your unsecured debts will be discharged,

and you will be relieved of all further plan payments. One advantage of converting from a 13 to a 7 is that all debts which you have acquired since you filed the 13 (called **post-petition** debts) can be included in your new Chapter 7 case. *In all other circumstances, post-petition debts are nondischargeable.* The problem with a 13 conversion is that non-exempt assets, otherwise protected in your 13 case, will be sold in your 7.

4. *Have the case dismissed.* In a very few cases, a dismissal might be preferable. A dismissal of the case puts the debtor and creditor back where they were before the case was filed (less any payments received). This may be preferable, for example, where a desirable non-exempt asset would be sold in a Chapter 7 conversion.

The Important Legal Concept to Remember: Chapter 13 plans are not easy to calculate. Once confirmed, all plan payments must normally be made to get a discharge.

AFTER
BANKRUPTCY

17

AFTER THE DISCHARGE

Discrimination

Attempts to collect discharged debts

Debts you forgot to list

Property you did not list

In a few cases, events that require action occur *after* the debtor has received his discharge.

DISCRIMINATION. It is flatly illegal for the government to discriminate against a debtor because that debtor went through bankruptcy.

> Pablo was a licensed general contractor who built office buildings. After his accountant embezzled $400,000 from his company, Pablo was forced to file Chapter 7. About a month after Pablo received his discharge, the State Contractors License Board wrote to Pablo and told him that it intended to revoke his contractor's license because of the bankruptcy. Pablo had his attorney write back, explaining that it is generally illegal to discriminate against a debtor because of a bankruptcy and specifically illegal to revoke, suspend, or refuse to renew a license or permit because of a bankruptcy. The matter was dropped shortly thereafter.

Again, the point of bankruptcy is to get a fresh start, and it would be very hard to do so if a government entity was able to hold the case against a debtor. It is illegal for the Department of Motor Vehicles to withhold a driver's license because of a debt that was discharged in bankruptcy (e.g., one created by a traffic accident). Similarly, parking tickets that are dischargeable in bankruptcy cannot form the basis for a denial of a driver's license. However, if the license is being withheld for reasons *unrelated to debt*—a bad driving record, for example—then there is nothing discriminatory about withholding a license.

The protection from government discrimination based upon bankruptcy is fairly broad. Federally guaranteed student loans or grants cannot be denied because of a bankruptcy filing. A transcript from a college cannot be withheld. It is illegal to deny someone accommodations in public housing or to otherwise deny government benefits or services (such as Social Security or welfare) because of a bankruptcy. Again, this protection is for discrimination based upon the filing of a bankruptcy or the discharge of a related debt; it offers no protection for denial of benefits premised upon other, unrelated, reasons.

Protection from discrimination also extends to private employers. It is illegal for an employer to discriminate against a person because that person filed bankruptcy. You cannot be fired if the reason for the firing is your bankruptcy. This is especially helpful where a Chapter 13 payment is automatically deducted from a debtor's paycheck (as sometimes happens), and the employer is unhappy about it.

A debtor who feels she has been illegally discriminated against because of a bankruptcy will need to bring a motion for sanctions against the transgressor in bankruptcy court.

ATTEMPTS TO COLLECT DISCHARGED DEBTS. Sometimes a creditor attempts to collect on a debt that was discharged. Creditors have absolutely *no right* to attempt to collect a discharged debt.

If one does, the first thing you can do is write a letter to the creditor explaining that his debt was discharged. Attach a copy of your discharge (*always keep the original in your files*), and tell him to stop it, or else. It is the "or else" that powers your letter. A discharge is a federal court order. In it, all creditors are specifically told to cease all further collection activities. Violating this order constitutes contempt of court and is illegal. Explain that to your creditor, and you should be left alone.

If you are not, you will need to go to court. A small claims action could result in a money judgment for a clear violation of the order. A smarter bet would be to file your action in your local bankruptcy court, since that is the court that issued the discharge order. Go to the clerk's office and ask about the proper procedure for bringing your complaint.

Remember this, though: debts not listed are debts not discharged. You must list the debt and the creditor in order to receive a discharge as to that debt. If you forgot to list a creditor whose debt would have been discharged had he been listed, see below.

As for debts that were not discharged—things like most taxes and student loans, child support and alimony, government fines, and so on—those creditors do have a right to get paid back once the case is concluded. There is nothing illegal about the IRS's garnishing your wages to get back taxes repaid, once your case is over.

Finally, what about secured debts that were neither reaffirmed, redeemed, nor surrendered?

Kathleen had listed a debt for a stove from Appliance Warehouse that she had bought three years before she filed bankruptcy. Although Appliance Warehouse had written to her during her case, requesting a reaffirmation, she never signed it and never gave the stove back. In fact, even though she stopped paying the debt, she never heard from Appliance Warehouse again.

Creditors with a legitimate security agreement retain their

interest in the property after the bankruptcy is over. The difference is that before the bankruptcy, the creditor had a security interest *and* you were personally liable for the debt. After the bankruptcy, although the creditor retains the security interest, your personal liability is discharged.

In Kathleen's case, her liability to Appliance Warehouse was wiped out with her discharge. Appliance Warehouse's only recourse after bankruptcy is to retake its three-year-old stove. How much will that cost Appliance Warehouse? More than the stove is worth? Probably. And what would they do with it? It is simply not cost-effective in many cases for a secured creditor to retake secured merchandise, depending, of course, upon the value of the merchandise.

And think about this: What if Appliance Warehouse does send two guys out to get the stove, but Kathleen refuses to let them into her house? In that case, Appliance Warehouse must hire a local attorney to go to state court and get an order allowing the store to come get its property. Now, how much will that cost? Ten times the value of the stove? That is why Kathleen never heard from Appliance Warehouse again.

Realize that the results would be different if it was a car that Kathleen decided to keep. In that case, the car would be rightfully repossessed soon after the discharge.

DEBTS YOU FORGOT TO LIST. Sometimes people forget to list a creditor on their schedules. Such debts are not discharged. If the mistake is discovered *before the case is over*, you can simply amend your schedules, pay a nominal fee to the bankruptcy clerk, file the amendment, and get the debt discharged.

If you discover the problem after you receive your discharge, then it is a bit more problematic. In that case, you will likely have to reopen your case and amend your schedules to get the debt discharged. This will require hiring an attorney and having a motion filed with the court.

Opening the case again will work only if your case was a no-asset case, that is, one in which everything you owned was fully exempt and there were no assets to distribute to your creditors. Most consumer Chapter 7 cases are no-asset cases. If yours was an **asset case**, it is unlikely that you will be allowed to reopen it. That is because the omitted creditor did not get to share in the proceeds from your assets, and the assets are already distributed. If that happened, you would still owe the creditor its money, as the debt would not have been discharged in your case.

One other option, instead of the costly and burdensome reopening the case choice, would be to write your creditor a letter. The Ninth Circuit Court of Appeals, for example, has stated that there is simply no need to reopen a case if the debt would have been discharged if it had been listed in the original filing. In the Ninth Circuit, the debt is treated *as if* it were discharged. In your letter, explain this to your creditor. In all likelihood, he will never know if you are in the Third District or the Eighth District or the Ninth District. And anyway, bluffing is not illegal.

PROPERTY YOU DID NOT LIST. If you forgot to list some property, and realized it after your case was discharged, you have an obligation to tell your trustee about it. You still might be allowed to keep it.

If the property would have been exempt had you listed it, the trustee will take no action and you can keep the property. Also, if the property is of no real value, the trustee will not take the time to reopen your case, take the property, sell it, and distribute the income to your creditors. Now, if you forgot to list that plot of land you own along the Carolina coast, you can rest assured that you will not own it for long.

In related matters, you have an obligation to tell the trustee about certain property you acquire *within 180 days after you file.* Those items are:

1. *Inheritances.* Whether by will or in a trust, any money you inherit within 180 days of filing becomes part of your bankruptcy estate.

2. *Death benefits.* This would include not only money received from life insurance, but proceeds from a death benefit plan as well.

3. *Divorce settlements.* Money or property received as a result of a divorce decree or a marital settlement agreement are part of your estate if received within 180 days of filing.

To the extent that any of these things are non-exempt, you may lose them to the trustee if he finds them to be of substance. This means that even if you filed your case on January 1, received your discharge on April 1, and inherited $10,000 on May 1, you would have to tell the trustee about the money.

The Important Legal Concept to Remember: Most people forget about their bankruptcy as soon as the discharge arrives. Normally, it is only when a creditor continues to pursue you, or you receive a substantial sum of money, that action after discharge is needed.

18

GETTING CREDIT AGAIN

Secured credit cards
Auto loans
Passbook loans
A mortgage?

There is no doubt that it will be more difficult for you to get credit again after your bankruptcy. That is a fact. But that does not mean it will be impossible. In fact, it is very possible. There are many creditors who still want your business. You can get credit again; it will just be more expensive this time around. Outlined below are several methods which will enable you to get that credit despite your bankruptcy.

SECURED CREDIT CARDS. Credit card companies do not trust some people, based upon their negative credit history, to repay money owed. In order to ensure payment, and get more business, they offer credit cards to these people *secured by some collateral*, specifically, by money. In exchange for a card with, say, a $250 credit limit, the credit card company requires that the applicant open up a bank account in the amount of $250 in its institution. If the cardholder fails to pay the money owed, the security will be used to pay the debt.

An important question to ask potential secured credit card

companies is whether the card is reported as secured to the credit reporting agencies. You want a card that is not reported as secured. Why? A secured card that is not reported as secured (and not all are) looks like it is unsecured on your credit report. Other potential creditors who read the report will be more inclined to give you unsecured credit if it *looks* like you have an unsecured credit already. You really begin to establish good credit again when you have unsecured credit.

Anyone, no matter how bad their credit history, should be able to get a secured credit card. They are offered by most banks, and can also be found in the classified sections of newspapers under "credit" or "money to lend."

AUTO LOANS. A debtor who is trying to reestablish credit should also check out a dealer-financed car loan. The key term to look for is "we carry our own papers." That means that the dealership does not use a bank to finance its used car loans. Instead, it finances the car itself. If you stop paying, it starts repossessing.

The problem with dealer-financed auto loans is the extraordinarily high interest rate one must pay. Whereas most new car loans may hover around 6 percent, a person with bad credit should expect to pay at least 20 percent. By comparison, a $10,000, 6 percent auto loan, if it were to be paid back in three years, would cost $11,800 (6 percent of $10,000 = $600; $600 × three years = $1,800; $10,000 + $1,800 = $11,800.) The same loan at 20 percent payable over three years would cost $16,000.

If this seems outrageous, that is because it is. But it is also an opportunity for people with bad credit to get a car and reestablish themselves financially. Once the loan has been paid back faithfully, it will be far easier for you to get a loan in the future. Not only will the interest rate be lower the next time, but more dealers will be interested in selling you a car.

PASSBOOK LOANS. This method is similar to, but also distinct from, the secured credit card procedure above. The idea is the same; use a savings account to establish credit. It's the execution that differs.

A passbook loan works like this: Take a fair amount of money, $500 for example, and open up a passbook savings account at a bank. Then ask the bank for a loan secured by your passbook savings account. It will give the money to you because the loan is secured by the savings account. Right off the bat you have gotten a major financial institution to give you a loan. That the loan is usually not reported as secured is icing on the cake. Anyone reading your credit report will be far more likely to extend you credit once they see that a conservative institution like a bank was willing to take a risk on you and lend you money.

A MORTGAGE? As strange as it may sound, it is quite possible to get a mortgage after you have received your discharge. It usually takes about two years of clean credit to get one.

For most people, it is quite a bit easier to pay bills in a timely manner after their discharge, and that is the key to getting a home loan after a bankruptcy. You need to have established a new history of *good* credit, instead of your old history of bad credit. Paying bills on time after your case is over, and using the techniques outlined above, will help make you a more attractive candidate to a lender.

Besides paying bills in full and on time, there are a few other things that may allow you to get a home loan after your case. The first is the knowledge on the part of lenders that very few people go through bankruptcy twice. Also, when you apply for a home loan, one of the main things a lender looks at is your debt-to-income ratio: how much you owe versus how much you bring home. Lenders want individuals with stable income and not too much debt. Well, guess what? After a bankruptcy, you have hardly any debt. If you are working, then your debt-to-income ratio is actually, surprisingly, quite good. With a new history of timely bill-paying, a mortgage can be had.

The Important Legal Concept to Remember: You can get credit again, once you know how.

19

STAYING OUT OF DEBT

Options besides going into debt
The need for a record
The need for a plan

OPTIONS BESIDES GOING INTO DEBT. Getting into debt was easy. Staying out of debt can be too. The very first trick to a life free from debt is nothing more than a simple change in attitude. In this society, debt is good. Consumers are constantly barraged to incur ever more debt; how else did you get all of those credit cards? And our national debt is over a trillion dollars. We are a nation of individual and institutional debtors.

What you need to do is change your attitude about debt. While you certainly did not want to get into as much debt as you did, *it must have been acceptable to you*, otherwise you would not have done it. The new attitude must be: *no more debt*.

Yes, the previous chapter was all about getting new credit. No one is telling you not to get credit again. Everyone needs credit. A (secured) credit card is necessary in this culture. To do something as mundane as cash a check in many places, you must have a credit card. To go on vacation and rent a car, you must have a credit card. Yes, you need credit.

But, do you need debt? Now there's the rub. Most people go into debt because their means do not justify their ends. They spend more than they make. Debt balances out the ledger sheet. But you need not go into debt this time around to balance your books. There are alternatives.

When you are short of money you have three options, not just one. Most people, when faced with a shortfall of cash, choose the first option—going into debt. But besides incurring more debt, another choice is to spend less. Maybe that sounds impossible; maybe you believe that you cannot spend any less than you do already. That might be true . . . and it might not. Read on to make sure. Again, staying out of debt requires a shift in your attitudes. Cutting back a bit and being debt-free *has to become more important* than buying that thing you want (or think you need).

Besides going into debt or cutting back, the last option when the books do not balance is to make more money. This too may seem impossible, but owing $50,000 probably seemed impossible at one time too. There is no shortage of money in this world. The trick is to get just a little bit more of it to flow your way.

None of this is to say you have to become a millionaire or a pauper to stay out of debt. It is just that going into debt is not the only way to solve a money crunch. If you are going to stay out of debt, then living within your means, either by making more or by spending less, *must take precedence over going into debt.*

THE NEED FOR A RECORD. Staying out of debt also requires that you know how much you spend every month.

Madeline vowed never to go through bankruptcy again. Her problem was that it seemed like every month, even after her discharge, she was about $200 short. She would take a cash advance or charge some groceries just to get by. Other than her rent and utility bills, she actually had no idea what she spent her money on every month. Before she could figure out how to live with what she made, she had to figure out where the money went.

It is kind of like that bumper sticker: "How can I be overdrawn? I still have checks left." Most people who go deeply into debt have no idea how much they spend on groceries, entertainment, clothes, or restaurants every month. Do you? If you don't, do you see how knowing this could be immensely helpful? That is the purpose of keeping a record.

Spend a month writing down, every day, exactly what you do with your money. How much is spent on food, cabs, gas, and magazines? Create categories, carry a little notebook with the categories listed, and keep a daily log of expenditures. If you are not keen on the notebook method, there are many personal-finance computer programs that allow you to do the same thing (and the graphs and pie charts are pretty dandy too). Either way, you need to begin to record every expenditure for at least one month.

List every little thing, *to the penny*: lunch, movies, books, dry cleaning, haircuts, everything. On days that you write large checks—rent, for example—enter those too. Twenty to thirty categories is not uncommon. Every time you spend money, put it in a category, or add a category. Your categories, the more specific the better, should also include:

- Rent
- Utilities
- Groceries
- Insurance
- Clothes
- Fast food
- Restaurants
- Entertainment (be specific)
- Transportation
- Medical
- Child care

· School expenses
· Health

At the end of the month, tally the results. The picture should be illuminating. Maybe you never knew that you spent $30 a month on late video charges. Maybe those $5 lunches added up. Whatever the case, this record will immeasurably help you see where the problem lies. To be really effective, keep the record for a few months.

> After dutifully recording her spending for a few months, the one thing that really surprised Madeline was how much she spent on fast food. Almost $300 was spent on burgers, fries, cokes, and snacks each and every month.

THE NEED FOR A PLAN. Once you see where things are, you can decide where you want them to be. You can decide that less needs to be spent on fast food, for example, or that more should be spent on entertainment. Instead of blindly spending whatever cash you have in your pocket on whatever need you may have on any given day, start your month by *planning ahead*. Right next to the totals on your record, put in a column for how much you plan to spend on each item the next month.

> Madeline decided that she could easily spend a lot less on fast food every month. Next to the $300 she had in that category's recorded total, she added a category called "Projected" and listed $150. On the first of the month, she went to the market and loaded up on her favorite items, and made sure to keep some with her each day as the month progressed. The very first month, she actually spent less than the $150 projected, and for the first time in a long time, she ended the month without a money crisis.

What this is not, is a budget. Budgets are like diets—they

don't work. What this is, is a plan of action. Budgets and plans are fundamentally different. A budget is a strict limit on what you cannot do. A plan is your choice as to what you want to do. Budgets are inflexible, plans are not; a plan can always be changed. Budgets control you, but you control your plans. The whole idea of the record and plan is to enlighten you and enable you to make intelligent decisions.

Again, when your books do not balance every month, you have three options: go into debt, spend less, or make more. Hopefully, going into debt again is no longer an option. Spending less is not that hard once you know where the money goes. After going through a bankruptcy, this should be easy. Good luck.

The Important Legal Concept to Remember: Staying out of debt need be no more difficult than a change of attitude, a record of expenses, and a plan of action.

VI

APPENDICES

COMMON QUESTIONS
AND ANSWERS

GETTING YOUR FINANCIAL HOUSE IN ORDER

Is there any advantage to using Consumer Credit Counseling instead of bankruptcy?
There are two. First of all, going through CCC will prevent a bankruptcy from going on your credit record. Second, the costs, when compared to paying legal and filing fees in bankruptcy, are much less. CCC is like a Chapter 13; you will repay your debts to your creditors over a period of time.

Can I sue a creditor who is harassing me?
Indeed. The Fair Debt Collections Practices Act specifically permits an individual to sue a collection agency for harassment. Small claims court is usually the best way to go. To win your case, you should use the "two P's"—preparation and proof. When presenting your case, you must be well prepared: be organized, and have all witnesses and evidence ready. You also need proof: witnesses, phone records, that sort of thing. It is when you are well organized and able to prove the harassment that you will get a judgment.

CHAPTER 7 PRE-FILING CONSIDERATIONS

I have lived with my boyfriend for five years and we have accumulated a lot of debt together. Can we file jointly?
No, only a husband and wife can file a joint bankruptcy.

I have a good credit rating, but my wife has a lot of debts and wants us to file Chapter 7 together. Should we both file?
It depends upon a couple of factors. If you have only been married a short while, then most of her debts are probably her separate debts (as opposed to joint debts). In that case, she can probably file without you. If you have been married for a while, then most of your debts are probably joint. Check to see whose name is on the credit application. In community property states, all debts incurred while married are joint debts, regardless of who applied for the credit. If your debts are joint, then you should file with her. If you do not, your creditors will come after you for repayment after her liability is extinguished.

One of my creditors told me that I had to have at least $10,000 in debts to file Chapter 7. Is that true?
No, it is not. In a Chapter 7, there is no minimum or maximum amount of debt. In a Chapter 13, you can have no more than $250,000 in unsecured debt and $750,000 in secured debt.

Will my employer find out about my bankruptcy?
It is possible, but not likely. A bankruptcy filing is a public document. Anyone can go down to the court and get a copy of your petition and schedules. Your employer will not, however, receive notice of your filing like all of your creditors will (unless you list your employer as a creditor). Note, though, that most communities list all bankruptcy filings for the week in a local newspaper, usually the local legal paper. Unless your employer reads these listings there is no reason why he should ever know about it.

Do I have to list the debt I owe my mother? I want to pay it, and I really don't want her to know about this.
You have an obligation to list all of your debts when you file for bankruptcy. Thus, you are required to list the debt you owe your mother. But even though the debt will get legally discharged, that does not mean that you may not have a moral obligation to repay the debt. Here is what you should do: 'fess up, list her, and tell her that you will pay the debt back nonetheless.

Do I have to list my credit cards that have a zero balance?
What you are required to do is list all of your creditors. If you have a credit card without any balance, then that card is not technically a creditor. Ostensibly, that creditor would never know about the case and you would then have a credit card with a zero balance with which to reestablish credit. On the other hand, computers "talk" to each other all the time now, especially with regard to money, so the unlisted credit card company may still find out about your bankruptcy and cancel the card.

I am afraid that someone will come into my home and check out my stuff if I file. True?
No one will come into your house (in fact, normally, the only person that can ever enter your home without your permission is a policeman with a court-issued warrant). It is also unlikely, though not impossible, that the trustee will run a credit or asset check on you. When you sign your bankruptcy paperwork, you do so under penalty of perjury, a $500,000 fine, and possible jail time should you lie. That is a pretty hefty incentive to tell the truth. If however, you have non-exempt assets, or you value an asset at a ridiculously low price, the trustee may ask to see the property.

Soon after I filed, I incurred a debt that I want to add to my bankruptcy. Can I do that?

No, you cannot. The date that you file your case is called your "petition date." Any debts that you incur after filing, called post-petition debts, cannot be added into your case. It is only debts incurred before you filed, called **pre-petition debts**, that can be discharged in your case.

CHAPTER 7 BANKRUPTCY

One of my utility companies requested a deposit after I filed my Chapter 7. I thought that was illegal.
What your utility company cannot do is to cut off service to you because you filed. However, a deposit for future service is legal, and future bills must be paid timely.

I owed my brother $5,000 and paid him off about a month before I filed. The trustee cannot get that money, can he?
Oh yes he can. Payments made to creditors within ninety days of filing are called preferential payments. Payments made to family, like this one, made in the year before filing are also considered preferential. The trustee can void the payment, get the money back, and then spread it around to your other creditors.

I am about to have $50,000 in debt discharged. Is that considered income for tax purposes?
Normally, the forgiveness of indebtedness is considered taxable income. Luckily for you, though, that is not true of debts discharged through bankruptcy.

All of my debts were discharged, but I continue to get bills from a couple of creditors. Should I sue?
In most instances, this is due to an oversight. Banks, department stores, and credit card issuers are all big corporations with many divisions. Sometimes one part of the company gets notice of the filing or discharge and it takes a while for the information to filter to the other parts of the company. All you need to do

is call up the company, tell them about your case, give them your case number, and request that all further communication cease. That should do the trick. A lawsuit would be laughed out of court.

My debts are huge—$350,000 in credit card debt and $800,000 in secured debt. What should I do?
You can always file a Chapter 7, but with so much debt, you presumably have a lot of non-exempt assets too. If you want to keep your property, you will need to file a Chapter 11, which is not unlike a much bigger and more expensive Chapter 13. You cannot file a Chapter 13 because you are over the permissible debt limits.

CHAPTER 13 BANKRUPTCY

I can no longer afford my plan payments. What will happen?
It is possible to amend your plan. If you can repay your unsecured creditors, over the course of the entire plan, what they would have received had you filed a Chapter 7, you still can get a discharge. Another option is to convert your case to a Chapter 7. The advantage of this is that any post-petition debts can be added into the new case, and discharged. If you do not do anything, the trustee will dismiss your case and you will not get any discharge.

Can I pay off my plan before the scheduled time set forth in my plan?
Yes, there is no penalty for that.

AFTER BANKRUPTCY

My employer found out about my bankruptcy and I was fired. What can I do?
It is specifically illegal, pursuant to the bankruptcy code, to fire an employee because of a bankruptcy. You will need to hire an attorney and file suit in bankruptcy court.

B

GLOSSARY

341 hearing: The hearing that the debtor must attend, at which the trustee and creditors may question the debtor about his assets and liabilities. Also known as the first meeting of creditors.

Amend: To alter or change.

Arrears/Arrearages: Money that is overdue and unpaid. The term usually applies to support payments and mortgages.

Asset case: A Chapter 7 case in which the debtor has non-exempt assets. Depending upon the unprotected property, the trustee typically takes the assets, sells them, and distributes the funds to the debtor's creditors.

Associate: A lawyer at a law firm who is merely an employee, and who is not a partner. Associates tend to be younger and less experienced than partners.

Automatic stay: The court order that issues automatically upon the filing of the case. The stay suspends all collection activities aimed at the debtor during the pendency of the case.

Bankruptcy: A federal court action designed to give debtors relief from indebtedness and a fresh start.

Bankruptcy court: A federal court, presided over by a bankruptcy judge, that is concerned exclusively with the administration of bankruptcy cases.

Bankruptcy estate: The total property of whatever kind owned by the debtor at the time of filing.

Bar association: An association of lawyers found on local, state, and national levels.

Chapter 7: The most common type of bankruptcy, especially for consumer debtors. In the typical Chapter 7, the debtor keeps the majority of his assets and has the majority of his debts discharged.

Chapter 13: Also known as a reorganization. Intended for use by debtors with a stable income and designed to allow for the repayment of some, if not all, of the debtor's debts.

Claim: Also known as a proof of claim, it is the form filed by a creditor demanding payment by the trustee.

Codebtor: Usually the co-signer or guarantor of a loan. Codebtors are equally liable for debts as the original debtor, and creditors have the right to collect payment from the codebtor if the debtor has the obligation discharged.

Collateral: Property that is pledged as security for the satisfaction of a debt; property subject to a security interest.

Collection agency: A business that attempts to collect a debt that the original creditor has either charged off or otherwise deemed uncollectable.

Complaint: The papers that initiate a lawsuit. A complaint sets forth the parties, the jurisdiction of the court, and the grounds upon which the suit is based, and requests that the court solve the problem by granting relief.

Confirm/Confirmation: Approval by the court of either a Chapter 11, 12, or 13 plan.

Consideration: The price, reason, or benefit that induces someone to enter into a contract. Usually, but not necessarily, money.

Contempt of court: Any act in willful disobedience of a court's authority. Failing to comply with a court order constitutes contempt of court.

Contract: An agreement between two or more parties based upon an offer, acceptance of that offer, and an exchange of money, goods, or services. A contract creates an obligation by the parties to do or not do something.

Convert/Conversion: The action whereby the debtor requests that his bankruptcy proceedings be changed from one chapter of the bankruptcy code to another. Conversions typically, but not necessarily, occur where an insolvent Chapter 13 debtor desires to change his case to a Chapter 7.

Credit: The ability of a person or business to borrow money, based upon a favorable opinion of the applicant by the potential lender.

Credit bureau: A business that investigates and keeps records of credit history. The information is then sold to interested parties.

Credit card fraud: Knowingly using a credit card without the intent to repay the debt. Charging $1,000 or more for cash, or luxury goods or items, in the sixty days preceding the filing of the bankruptcy is presumed to be credit card fraud. Large charges outside that time frame may also be considered fraudulent, depending upon the circumstances.

Creditor: A person to whom a debt is owed.

Credit report: The report on a person's credit history, issued by a credit bureau.

Debtor: The person who owes money to creditors. One who files a bankruptcy case.

Deficiency balance: The amount of money, if any, that a debtor owes a creditor after the creditor sells the secured property it has retaken from the debtor.

Discharge: The order of the bankruptcy court that releases the debtor from his legal obligation to repay all dischargeable debts. Once a debt has been discharged, the debtor no longer legally owes the money to the creditor.

Dismiss: In bankruptcy, to dispose of the case without granting a discharge of debts.

Emergency filing: Filing only the petition and list of creditors in order to get the automatic stay ordered. Normally used to forestall a foreclosure or other collection activity.

Equity: The value of property once all debts have been subtracted from its worth.

ERISA: The Employee Retirement Income Security Act. The name refers to a pension or retirement plan that fits this federal designation.

Exemption planning: The process whereby the debtor transforms non-exempt assets into exempt assets in order to protect the property from the reach of the trustee.

Exemptions: The individual state and federal laws that detail how much and what kind of property a debtor may keep.

Fair Credit Reporting Act (FCRA): Federal law that regulates credit bureau activity.

Fair Debt Collections Practices Act (FDCPA): Federal law that regulates collection agencies.

Fair market value: The amount that a willing buyer would pay a willing seller for a piece of property.

File: The process whereby the debtor (or his agent) brings the bankruptcy petition and schedules to the bankruptcy clerk's office, and pays the filing fee. Upon filing, the automatic stay is issued immediately.

Filing fees: The amount the debtor must pay to have his petition and schedules filed in the bankruptcy court.

First meeting of creditors: The hearing that the debtor must attend, at which the trustee and creditors may question the debtor about his assets and liabilities. Also known as a 341 hearing.

Flat fee: A payment arrangement wherein the exact fee is set and will not be raised or lowered.

Foreclosure: An action whereby a secured creditor forces the sale of the collateral that was used to secure the loan. Used when a debtor fails to pay a debt in a punctual manner. A creditor remedy normally used to cure real property defaults.

Fraud: A false representation of the truth that is intended to induce another to act or rely upon the falsehood. A fraud may result from lying, omitting the truth, or concealing the truth.

Fresh start: As contemplated by the bankruptcy code, it is the purpose of bankruptcy.

Garnishment: A court-ordered method of debt collection whereby the debtor's wages are withheld to pay the debt.

Gross value: The value of property without subtracting any liens or other indebtedness. What the property would sell for.

Home equity loan: A home loan that provides the debtor with a loan amount equal to his equity in the property. The amount of the loan is then added into the overall indebtedness on the property. The new indebtedness may become part of the first mortgage, or may create a new second (or even third) mortgage.

Homestead/Homestead exemption: Laws passed in most states allowing a homeowner to protect his house in bankruptcy. Each state has different limits on the amount of equity in the home that can be protected.

Indebtedness: The total amount of debt owed by the debtor.

Judgment: The official and final decision of a court at the end of a trial.

Judgment lien: After a party succeeds in a lawsuit, it is a lien put on the property of the loser in order to eventually collect on the judgment.

Levy: The legal process whereby property is seized and sold, or where money has been attached.

Lien: An encumbrance or claim upon property used to secure payment of a debt. Once the debt is paid, the lien is removed. If the debt is not paid, any sale of the property will first be used to remove the lien and satisfy the debt.

Lien avoidance motion: A motion brought by the debtor to avoid certain sorts of liens that impair the debtor's exemptions.

Litigation: The adversarial legal process whereby one party sues another to right an alleged wrong.

Matrix: The list of all creditors, in alphabetical order, filed with the petition and schedules, used to mail notice of the case to those creditors.

Motion: A request made before a court that asks the court to rule on a matter in a certain way.

No-asset case: A Chapter 7 case in which all assets of the debtor are fully exempt.

Nondischargeable debts: Those debts that are not dischargeable in bankruptcy.

Nondischargeability complaint: A complaint filed by a creditor in the bankruptcy court requesting that its debt not be discharged along with the rest of the debtor's dischargable debts. The complaint must allege a reason for the request, usually some sort of fraud.

Non-exempt assets: Those assets, owned by the debtor, that are over and above, or otherwise not protected by, the exemption limits of the state. Non-exempt assets can be seized and sold by the trustee.

Order: The final decision by a judge with regard to a matter before the court.

Paralegal: A legal aide who has some knowledge of the law, but who is not a lawyer.

Perjury: Lying under oath. Perjury is a crime.

Personal property: All property other than real estate. It usually connotes money and goods.

Petition: The first two pages of a bankruptcy. The petition lists the debtor's name, address, Social Security number, and other necessary information.

Plan: In a Chapter 13, it is the debtor's blueprint for paying off his debts within a certain number of months.

Post-petition debts: All debts incurred after the filing of the petition.

Pre-petition debts: All debts incurred before the filing of the petition.

Presume/Presumption: To assume a fact beforehand.

Principal: The amount of the debt, not including interest.

Priority debts: Debts that must be paid first, pursuant to the bankruptcy code.

Pro per: A debtor who files his bankruptcy without the assistance of an attorney.

Purchase money security interest: A loan whereby the item purchased secures the loan.

Reaffirmation: An agreement whereby a debtor agrees to become liable anew for a debt that would otherwise be discharged in bankruptcy.

Real property: Land, and usually whatever is built upon the land.

Redemption: An agreement whereby a debtor agrees to purchase secured merchandise from a creditor for the current fair market value of the item, instead of what is owed.

Relief from stay: A motion brought by a secured creditor in bankruptcy court, in order to continue collection activities.

Reorganization: Another name for a Chapter 13 case.

Repossession: The action taken by the creditor to reclaim the property after a debtor defaults on a loan, typically an automobile loan.

Retention: The process, allowed in certain states, whereby a debtor keeps a secured item, keeps making payments, but signs no new reaffirmation agreement.

Schedules: The lists of assets and liabilities of the debtor, attached to the petition, that comprise the bulk of the bankruptcy filing.

Second mortgage: A mortgage that is subordinate to the primary mortgage. In the case of a default, the first mortgage is repaid before the second mortgage by the proceeds of the sale of the property.

Secured debt: A debt protected by collateral.

Seizure: The act of taking possession of property.

Settlement: An adjustment between two or more parties, resolving differences.

Small claims court: A special court that provides informal, quick, and inexpensive resolution of small matters. The limit is usually under $5,000, although it varies from state to state.

Statement of intention: One page of the bankruptcy paperwork wherein the debtor states his intention with regard to his secured property.

Sue: To commence a legal proceeding.

Surrender: To return secured property to the lender.

Tools of the trade: Implements, tools, books, and other items used by the debtor in his trade or profession.

Trustee: A person, appointed by the Department of Justice, who administers the bankruptcy case and estate for the benefit of the debtor's creditors.

Unsecured debt: Debt not associated with any sort of collateral.

Wild card: An exemption available under the federal system, as well as most state systems, that can be used to protect any property owned by the debtor, up to the wild card limit.

C

HOMESTEAD EXEMPTIONS FOR EACH STATE

The following is an abbreviated version of each state's homestead exemptions. *It is intended for overview only, and should not be used to actually calculate schedule C (Property Claimed As Exempt), as the specific laws are far more complex than listed here, they are periodically changed, and the necessary analysis is far more complicated.* It is also important to note that Congress may enact a federal law that supersedes these states limits in the not too distant future.

In some states, the amount of the exemption can be doubled if the debtors are husband and wife and are filing together. Other states limit the amount of land that can be protected.

STATE	AMOUNT	DOUBLE?	LIMIT
Alabama	$5,000	Yes	160 acres
Alaska	$54,000	No	None
Arizona	$100,000	No	None
Arkansas	Unlimited, if head of household	No	.25 acre city, 80 acres rural
California	$50,000 if single; $75,000 if married; $100,000 if 55 or older and	No	None

	earn less than $15,000 a year; $100,000 if 65 or older or physically or mentally disabled		
Colorado	$30,000	No	None
Connecticut	$75,000	No	None
Delaware	None	No	None
District of Columbia	None	No	None
Florida	Unlimited	No	.5 acre city 160 acres rural
Georgia	$5,000	No	None
Hawaii	$30,000 if head of household or over 65; $20,000 everyone else	No	1 acre
Idaho	$50,000	No	None
Illinois	$7,500	Yes	None
Indiana	$7,500	No	None
Iowa	Unlimited	No	.5 acre city, 40 acres rural
Kansas	Unlimited	No	1 acre city, 160 acres rural
Kentucky	$5,000	No	None
Louisiana	$15,000	No	160 acres
Maine	$12,500; $60,000 if over 60, or physically or mentally disabled	Yes	None
Maryland	None	No	None
Massachusetts	$100,000; $200,000 if over 65 or disabled	No	None
Michigan	$3,500	No	1 lot city, 40 acres rural
Minnesota	$200,000; $500,000 if primarily agricultural	No	.5 acre city, 160 acres rural
Mississippi	$75,000; higher if over 65 and married or widowed	No	160 acres
Missouri	$8,000	No	None
Montana	$40,000	No	None
Nebraska	$10,000	No	2 lots city, 160 acres rural
Nevada	$125,000	No	None
New Hampshire	$30,000	No	None

New Jersey	None	No	None
New Mexico	$30,000, but only if married, widowed, or supporting another	Yes	None
New York	$10,000	Yes	None
North Carolina	$10,000	No	None
North Dakota	$80,000	No	None
Ohio	$5,000	No	None
Oklahoma	Unlimited	No	Only if less than .25 acre
	$5,000	No	If more than .25 acre city, or 160 acres rural
Oregon	$25,000 if single; $33,000 if married	No	1 block city, 160 acres rural
Pennsylvania	None	No	None
Rhode Island	None	No	None
South Carolina	$5,000	Yes	None
South Dakota	Unlimited	No	1 acre city, 160 acres rural
Tennessee	$5,000 if single; $7,000 if jointly owned	No	None
Texas	Unlimited	No	1 acre city, 100 acres rural if single, 200 acres rural if married
Utah	$8,000; add $2,000 per spouse and $500 per dependent	No	None
Vermont	$30,000	No	None
Virginia	$5,000; add $500 per dependent	No	None
Washington	$30,000	No	None
West Virginia	$7,500	No	None
Wisconsin	$40,000	No	None
Wyoming	$10,000	No	None

The current federal homestead limit is $15,000, and may be doubled for married couples filing jointly. It is scheduled to be raised every three years.

INDEX